metaphors and muses

Saif Madre

INDIA • SINGAPORE • MALAYSIA

ISBN 979-8-88883-912-6

Contents

perhaps we are all poetries

perhaps we all are poetries
rhymed differently under the sun
we are poetries, short and long ones
vague sometimes
and somedays too deep to interpret
we are poetries in parts
and poetries incomplete.
we are poetries of the beating hearts
falling in love, holding hands
or we are poetries of those who fall apart
reeking of closure on jagged branches
we are poetries on the last pages
of notebook that gets lost away
we are poetries to be found
and treasure in souls that sway
we are poetries perhaps that you never recite
or poetries they chant more than prayers
we are poetries beautiful to be read
and even poetries capable of bloodshed.

—**Saif Madre**

you feel a lot like love

you feel a lot like love when i hold your hands, and the warmth of you grips me to reality. it's not always that one finds a way out of the paradigm of misery and agony, but i wonder if it's good fortune that i did, or was it the long for your touch that pulled me out of my misery. the clouds ask me often, if it's because of you that the rain doesn't trouble me anymore, if it's because of you that i am happy nowadays.

you feel a lot like love when you inhabit my mind. is it healthy when somebody takes total control on your thoughts, your mind? if not, tell it to my mind, for it's only your face that i see when i close my eyes, that now all my lips can spell are the syllables of your name. it feels like a sin to not think about you, that a thought that doesn't end up to you would conveniently be of no use. tell everything to my mind who now holds no regard for anything, anyone but you.

you feel a lot like love when our eyes meet each other. the intimacy that the moment holds has such value that words would never be capable to uphold. one look and everywhere i go i think about you. you make me wonder, if forever is ever true? for it would be a scary thought to not look at those eyes someday. for your eyes are now the saving grace for the chaos in mine.

you feel a lot like love when you call out my name. it feels as if, your voice is of the sirens, silencing all around it, so all that reaches my ears is you spelling my name in slow words, dipped in honeycomb. you get me mesmerized, call it witchcraft or my failing resistance to your undying love. so forgive me when i fall victim to you, forgive me as i turn red when you say, "all the love stories begins with i, ours will end with us."

you feel a lot like love when you smile. perhaps it's the way your cheeks redden with a hint of love, or maybe how your eyes scrunch up to little orbs of glowing stars but a glimpse of your infamous smile makes me want to live a day more. i have now recognized you as my home, one where the world falls short and where all roads leads to ultimately. for now the verses tattooed on my ribs end with your name and the mere sight of you is enough serotonin for a lifetime. for now you don't just feel like love, rather you are.

—Saif Madre

haven't we all heard?

haven't we all heard
that sinners never go to heaven
for they throw all the bad stones
in the dark pits of hell; hotter than the sun.
but wouldn't then heaven be scarce?
since sinning is all humanity knows
in oblivion or total awareness,
sinning is how we grow.
there are curses branded on our chest
swear words on the edge of our tongues
our eyes burn the rage of achilles
our hearts suffering the fate of patroclus.
our utopia is a paradox
for the miserable existential dread
but dare it challenge our crippled sanity
albeit being mere moments away from dead.
there is a visceral ache in all of our bodies
that we hide under a visible pretense
guilt; an anchor to our humanity

and regret, the path to make amends.
but i wonder if the redemption is sacred?
for all of our ghosts in veils
or if we are doomed to an eternity
of our pitiful existence in hell.

—**Saif Madre**

this hanging apocalyptic symphony

days goes by, weeks are limping
my words are forgotten
lips burnt by the flames
of what seems to be thy name.
my grief is like a mouth
toothless and gasping for breath
my anxiety looks to burst out
in closed spaces, cages and nets.
i am disfigured, beyond recognition
hidden from the world, one eye swollen shut
the other in search of random if's and buts.
i wonder what colour is January
if not the seamless blue of tragedy
coldness brewing in hearts
spitting on unfinished art.
i am living inside a mirror
disgusted by my own face
i am trying to cope up with myself

of all the strangest of ways.
i have figured i am lost
in the heap of my dirty laundry
trying to find an escape out
of this hanging apocalyptic symphony.

—**Saif Madre**

i am homesick yet not sure what home is

my wrist taps on the kitchen table, and the hollow sound that echoes through the empty room stays. it magnifies till my ear bleeds red out of resounding grief and bottled remorse. the chair next to me has dust on the surface for no one has sat on it for a long time. the plates in the sink remain unwashed for my mother trusted me with them and all i know is to inflict disappointment on others. my father is away afar the seas, earning money for my comfort but only if the green bits of paper provided any warmth. and while this loneliness is unwelcome, it's all i have got.

my friends call me a liar everytime i give them excuses for not coming up with them. well they're not wrong but how else do i explain to them that while my heart craves for love and belonging, a mere depiction of it by somebody rattles by bones and gives me goosebumps. every praise in my name stays in my head, inhabited for eternity. my stale blood clears up, the hurricane in my abdomen seems to clear up on the thought that i wouldn't be so translucent to everyone. but i am afraid of the peace, for the unsettling chaos in my mind is what i am only familiar to.

here's an obvious tip, if you are searching for graves inside cemeteries, you're going to find ghosts. but not always in the white veils and with the sunken bloodshot eyes. ghosts might just be transparent who latch on your bodies and pull out your long hidden insecurities. the never-looked-at insecurities would then illuminate your grief like a beacon shining amongst the dark clouds raining over you. they would make you loathe your life, make you question your existence and pity the dead so much that you'd want to be a labyrinth forthcoming lullabies of eulogies.

my wardrobe hides a lots of secrets but all of them fall inferior to the abundance of books i never read. i am well aware of the mess i have made in an attempt to make a library of my own but to read the words floating, guilty of creating an abstract kingdom of fictional soldiers wielding wisdom. have i grown cozy in the world i made oblivious of the moving reality? perhaps yes, but i behold no shame to look for an abode in not people but verses and reigning metaphors. for books is where you find a home for the stray and lost.

tell me, if it's alright to feel lost. to feel away from the typical emotions of love and affection while it's being presented to you on a platter. i have wrung my heart in an attempt to find traces of any likes of humanity, any benign sympathy for those i have ghosted in the wake of my disappearance. i have washed the dishes now for there was nothing to do and the white noise in my head nibbled on my sanity that appears to be falling apart. i have locked the rooms despite there is no one who would wish to enter in my abode of endless despair. i have hidden my father's gifts under the blanket for his redemption is no more needed. slowly the loneliness is grown to me, welcomed, embraced. for there is no home left to look for if not the solitude i lay in.

—Saif Madre

"do you love me?"

"do you love me?"

"huh?"

"do you love me?"

"didn't i tell you yesterday that i love you?"

"yes, but do you still love me?"

you don't answer me and the silence sends me down a spiral of thoughts. you speak after a minute and it perks up my ears but all you say is, "switch off the lamp." i ask you if you're okay and you ask me if i trust you still. i nod when i want to say it's not me i trust, it's not the demons growing in me biting on my flesh and confidence i trust. but i nod and that's all i do.

it's midnight and i wake up for a glass of water. and i hear whimpered sounds, groans of misery. for once it's not me making that sounds and i hear them coming from you. i stare at you holding my breath and i ask if i did anything wrong. you say it's not my fault

but my mind tells me otherwise. i wait for you to tell me you need me but you don't, so i go to sleep. next day you've left, and all that's on the other side of bed is severe emptiness and the scent of you.

it's not that i am surprised of you leaving, i always knew you'd someday for you had a million reasons to leave. but it's what you said on that tattered piece of paper by the dining table. "it's not you, it's me" how easily you blamed yourself while it was evident it was my insecurities that swallowed what we had. was it what you call a closure so i wouldn't plummet myself to death in the memories of you? was that why you lied?

it's strange how adapted we have grown to lies, that the truth seems too bitter to say.

i visited the grocery store today to buy your favourite cereals and peanut butter. the shack in the kitchen lies as a souvenir of you. i sleep keeping the lights on, afraid that if you'd return, i couldn't see you in the dark. i turn around the aisle and i spot you with someone buying croissants and i see you happy like you were never with me. you are wearing my favourite shade of blue and i want to ask you why you never wore it when you went out with me, though it's not my place to ask, neither is thinking of you as often as i do. i want to walk up to you and i wonder if the world is vast or small because you're standing 6 feets from me and it feels miles from where we are. but the demons in my mind tell me to let go of the urge and let her be happy. happy without me.

i am sitting at terrace, under the blanket of stars thinking of you. i do that often as you know. i am thinking how the things that make people love you can also be the things that make them unlove you. i think of how you loved my voice then, that the poetries i recited for you were the sonnets of heaven for you, but as time passed all you heard from me were faint cries. i think how my arms was your go-to place, a place to cry and cherish, how you called it home but when was it when you started suffocating among them?

i walk up to the edge of terrace, with closed eyes and the ground doesn't seem too far. i try to reach to it but someone pulls me back. was it you? i open my eyes and the eerie silence striked again. but it's different now, the scent of you is faint now and perhaps the gods watching over me has granted me some mercy over the agony of losing you. days have passed but now my closet doesn't reek of you and i realize how there is more space for me on the bed. but the peace is short lived as i get a text from you,

"do you love me still?"

and inspite myself, i respond,

"huh?"

—**Saif Madre**

by the name of you

stars whisper your name to me
saying how love starts by your name
and ends with syllables of mine
they tell me how the worlds are colliding
and we are the collateral damage
still the clasped fingers never separate.
the stars inform me of despair to come
and how you're a bad omen
but misfortune is my kin
and i'd better be stranded
rather than away from you
for what good is luck
if you're the wish that remains incomplete.
stars tell me of all the fingers you've crossed
all 11:11's you waited for
only to embrace me in your arms
and how when everything falls apart
you still search of new ways to love me
the stars ask me if it's worth it

to let you ruin me
in the most gruesome way possible
and i say in undignified certainty
how in the end chaos anyway surrounds us
but this peace will pertain
by the name of you.

—**Saif Madre**

all the tender words you said to me

"you look like moon in a satin dress"

it was long ago that i had smiled wide, careless before today. it always took great efforts to feel good about myself before i met you. i was always the silent, shy kind until you came along and now chaos prevails in my mind. so when you look at me and tell me about the beauty you see in my eyes, i believe it. i believe you for your face would betray the love you hold for me even if you never say it outright.

"this reminded me of you"

you text me bits of love by writers renowned for their fables and tell me how you want it all with me, just not in fiction. everytime you take my name, my insides churn in anticipation of you, for to believe you know me, remember me even in my absence feels to good to be real. you whisper to me, "if i was a supervillain, faced by a choice to choose you or a conspiracy, i wouldn't think twice before taking you with me, for you are the sin even god would forgive me for." and i look at you, helpless, so helpless in love.

"you mean the world to me"

the mere words could feel as if an over exaggeration, a writer's play with the wonders of words. but when you tell me this, i see how your eyes scrunch up tight, how your smile creases at right angles. i see how no other honest man could compete with the truthfulness in your voice. you clasp our hands together and i feel the warmth of universe beneath our fingers, one you kept apart for me, for eternity seems bearable with you.

"daisies bloom at the sight of you"

oh, do you remember that day when the destiny held beef against me and it felt easy to fall apart then keep holding the strings putting me together? do you remember the grin on your face as i never seemed to stop ranting at minor inconveniences in my life? i had hit you for laughing at me but couldn't resist giving in to the laugh either. i asked whether you thought if i was a bad person, and you told me that while it was evil of me to take your share of pizza slice, i was otherwise the sunshine that brightened your day, the art that never let your life go bland.

"i would choose you in every lifetime"

promises often seem debatable to me, the idea of a said forever torn at seams, the i love you's a little bitter at the end. but with you, i have seen how you have lived upto what you say, how your actions weigh more than any promise to be made. your lips pour reassurance on the burns of my insecurities with no hesitation at all. so let it be love in slow motion or flaws crippling us apart, i seem to have found a home in you, one i'd inhabit with no regrets whatsoever.

—Saif Madre

Have you ever realised?

Have you ever realised?
How quickly time passes
For I feel it was just yesterday
When I was 3, and crying my heart out
And no one judged my masculinity.
And then moments later
I was 6, as everyone told me
I could be anything I want,
But I guess opting for science was silent.
A few birthday cakes later
I aged to 10 years
And I finally acquired the fear of death
As I learnt the untold secret.
I walked with comics in hand
To 13, with pimples sprouting
On my already ugly face
And realised, it hurts
Being backstabbed by friends
Who promised forever.

Stealing glances at my crush
I slumped into 16,
And I learnt finally
How to put feeling born within silences into words
So I wrote about language of flowers
And guilt haunting my conscience
At 2 am, while, I lay on my tear stained pillow.
A couple of months to 17
But the gifts and parties don't excite me
Anymore except for the chocolate cake
That I will always look forward to.

—**Saif Madre**

Step by step guide to finding home in a person

i. Stop looking

Watching others fall in love and float in it does arise the want in us to share such feelings, such affection with someone. It's not abormal to crave to be someone's ardent desire. But don't go to library's to stumble upon someone. Maybe Bollywood doesn't work in real life. Maybe "Kehte hai agar kisi cheez ko dil se chaaho...to poori kaynat usse tumhe milane ki koshish mei lagjaati hai" doesn't really work in reality. Maybe you wouldn't even know when love's around, until it pounces on you. Maybe love will strike when you least expect it to.

ii. Ask questions. A lot of them.

Love tiptoes in our lives many times. Some in ocean blue eyes and raven hair, some nervous to even utter words of empathy, some hopeless, awkward and desperate for love. And maybe all of them are real, nevertheless how they ended, but just didn't fit with you like you wanted. Ask questions to the potential lovers who churn your insides and who make the butterflies in your stomach flutter. Ask them if the promises they make come with an expiry date, if their fingers would cling hands other than yours someday, if you're the muses of the poems they write. Ask questions before love really does make you blind.

iii. Are the silences comfortable?

Let's assume you find what you call the love of your life, and the vase in your house now bear flowers you didn't buy or the hoodies in your wardrobe are lesser than before. But would you really call it love when you have spent the words to talk on, and your sinful eyes would catch their gaze, sputtering for words so the aura of communication doesn't die, suffocating you in a hazardous awkward silence. Or do you just sit around, doing nothing, but looking at each other. You read, they write, and you sit in silence, waiting for something more, one that is cozy, where words are lazy, and eyes sunken and weary on looking at them with longing. Maybe then, you would walk a step closer to the home you wish to live in.

iv. The bad parts of it

Are you aware that just like water, after love warms, it boils? For as much as we would want it to be, all the beautiful things aren't just pure. But the very darkness in them allows it to be enchanting. We humans tend to be attracted to what destroys us, keep us up at nights, pick out our insecurities by fingers and dangles them in front of us. There mights be arguements and such, maybe by a third person guilty of it or maybe you would fair well in the disagreements by yourself. But after a long day, would you pick out flowers for yourself or lay in their arms, conversing of the mutual dilemmas in a humane manner, one that didn't dawn upon you earlier. Would you let go, or hold on tighter?

v. Long distance or a short love?

Distance makes the heart fonder as you've heard. But those five words would prick your skin in places you never fathom could hurt, when the one you wished to embrace, keep besides you for the long eternity, is away from your hands reach. All you could think of, would be of them, counting days on your fingers till your eyes would meet with them. Every face reminding of their features, the connect between both held together by telephone wires.

Your pillow would know of the yearn you clutch on, waiting as the days pass and the stars dim to nothing. Your life would seem nothing more than a sad tale of a playwright, and of the time you stay apart, you would come to realize how missing is the same as loving.

vi. Finally, confession?

Was it made beforehand? Did it slip from between the tongue when you held their hand and maybe it felt like the right time, when you felt reckless, knowing it was very unlike you. You did it right, if your eyes aren't embedded with tears of sorrow, if not yet there's a time you would know. Take them to where your hearts fit right, maybe under a blue sky of pure white stars where you'd tell them how you want them to be your star-crossed love, or in the rusty cafe smelling of amortentia, or in your home in shorts and smelling like a corpse dying for their love(too cheesy, is it?) Tell them of your feelings for them, all they made you feel, and how after wandering for long you found a home in them. For in the end, you would know better of your love, wouldn't you?

—Saif Madre

"Why do you fear the stars?"

"Why do you fear the stars so much?" she whispered against my closed eyelids.

"I don't fear them." I told her, keeping my gaze away from the sparkling celestial.

"Aren't you aware, you can't lie to me."

"I'm not trying to. Just evading the truth for a bit." I chuckled to which she returned a grin.

"Does the starry sky gives you butterflies?"

"Yes, but not more than you." I said, smiling.

"You can open your eyes, you know?"

"I don't want to. I'm scared."

"I'm there for you." I smiled, glad she didn't question my irrational fear towards stars.

"Do we like...hold hands now?" She asked, while I sat besides her, up on the tower's terrace.

I clasped my hand into her. And opened my eyes.

"When my father died, they told me he would reappear as a star. I looked out, every day, to find glimpes of him, trying to recognize which one of the constellations, matched his wisped eyebrows and the cigar he sported."

She looked at me, with glinting eyes, hinting that she had taken interest in my words.

"I talked to the sky, waiting, listening to the moon and her miseries. I fell in love with the night, and forgot what I ever looked for. My father became a hazy memory, of a past left long behind. It felt the stars were shining, just for me. Until it fell apart. All of it."

"What...what happened?" She asked, concerned.

"I fell asleep right there. Out in the garden once. And there was none, who paid witness to my mother suffocating for breath, except for my helpless brother who couldn't help but cry for help, but alas! None heard."

"It wasn't your mistake. You were mourning."

"Was I? I should've been over it already."

"You couldn't control it. It's not in your hands."

"I wish it was. I wish the stars would let me be, the moon leaving for being lonely as I ever was. That the sky wouldn't make promises that I belonged. I am scared to fall for the rain again, that washed away my sufferings. I don't want to look at the sky again, and want to find my father. You shouldn't love the dead too long, or you might start killing the one's living."

She didn't say anything. But stood up, and pulled me too. We walked over the ledge, as far as I could assume. I wouldn't have minded if she threw me over, sent me to join the wide sky, I thought but resurfaced my thoughts, afraid of a blind love reinstating the old, forgotten memories. She took a step towards me, kissed me as I opened my eyes and I could taste heaven on the tip of my tongue. She stared at me and whispered,

"The stars wouldn't intrigue you as much, if you love the living enough."

—Saif Madre

Aftermath of death

12 November 2016, 4:23 pm

It's a little cold. Not the breezy cold, that makes you pull on the hems of your sweater. Cold like loneliness has gripped me, denying to leave unless it engulfs me whole and I don't even resist. Cold like I have been thrown in a void, a botomless pit and I don't try to escape. But graveyards are as cold as they can be. And to look at the helpless corpse of your dead mother doesn't ease the pain. It fuels the pain rather.

13 November 2016, 3:11 am

I cannot sleep. I have stranded thoughts that I have tried to avoid, but the very attempt to do so makes me think about them. What would my life be like, I wonder, but the thought scares me beyond measure. I choke on my own tears, trying to reach out for her, but my hands flail in empty air. I wish for mere hallucinations of her, to see her at least in glimpses, for sanity is the last thing I need.

20 November 2016, 6:51 pm

It's been a week. A week since she took her own life, oblivious to the chaos she has left behind. The chaos that's me. All the grief, sorrow it has turned into rage, endless rage wrecking havoc all within me. I feel helpless, but I try not to show it. The fates have decreed me to survive

But what do you do, when survival feels cruel?

The invisible scars on my vulnerability have poked holes in my soul, and my life is escaping through it. I am tired of pretence, i am tired of existence.

12 November 2017, 1:01 am

A year, isn't it? Tell me, how do you celebrate death anniversaries? Are red roses okay for someone who loathed red? She told me how it is impure, unholy. When I asked her, what about the blood running in our veins, she moved away. But maybe now I realize that it was the very blood that rooted the hatred for red. I was her blood too. Did she hate me? Was I why she never woke up that day? I wonder if she misses me still like I miss her.

26 March 2018, 8:48 pm

I wrote my first poetry today. Recited it too in front of a crowd. There were hoards of claps and words of appreciation, but the only proud eyes I searched for were hers. It's been a long time. But it still hurts.

07 July 2019, 5:23 pm

I visited her grave again. And I believed since long, that I was over her. That my heart had healed, that it wouldn't heart to stand over her grave, and talk about sweet nothings. But the hurt seems infinite, and I feel I'm on the first page again, helpless and suffering in eternal agony.

22 February 2020, 10:11 am

It still hurts. A lot.

ode to a lover

i wanna love you till it hurts me
till it tears me apart
in shreds and pieces
because love is destructive
it breaks bones more than hearts
but it's the only way out of the labyrinth
that seems to have captured me
in addled minds and insane souls
and only way out is pain
pain that grants no mercy
pain that you call love

cut my heart out
and sew it to yours
for its jumping in my chest
rattling the ribcage
in endless chaos
just for a glimpse of you
and what better way there could be
to be intimate in this world

with stone hearts and frozen vulnerabilities
than to hand mine to you
with an exchange of vows
because you are my better half
a part of me that I wish never falls apart

my fingers seemed too less
to count all our forevers
for my hands are exhausted
at eight almosts that we could never fulfill
and yours fingers have swollen
reciting out the beautiful distractions
made of you and me
but i wonder if it ever will be over
as you're the muse to my ink
and my ink denies to be left alone
until it paints all the intricate details of you
on the white canvas of me
fortunate as i ever could be

aren't we both castaways?
striving to survive
longing to belong
you look at me with pleading eyes
with hints of anguish and misery
reflecting the helplessness in mine
we never were the ones

to meet under the misletoe
dancing with arms wrapped around each other
we lay amid the stormed sorrow
waiting for the lightning to strike us apart
for in no other way
we would let each other go.

—**Saif Madre**

aren't we all a little hungry for love?

you'd twirl in the rain,
a smile from your amor,
and voila, you've become a puddle,
it's a feast you cannot enjoy.
a feeling you cannot comprehend.
it'll leave you hanging, hollow.
after the eternally ephemeral promises,
aren't we all a little hungry for love?

love, a lie, everlasting truth, you decide. a fleeting touch, a glance of yearning, a hug lest the world consumes you. it is that perdurable feeling, one that lingers after aeons if true. perhaps orchestras do play the ephemeral symphony, the world bursts forth in colour, the heart ceases to beat, one's whole being comes to a standstill. well, how would i know? i am a mere dreamer, and it is not often that fiction written in the pages of a draft or screenplay acts out in life.

love, i believe, is a lot of things. love is destruction and love is redemption. love has thorns but it would be impossible to neglect it's petals. love is pity and still appears to be ruthless. love is the grey where we all persist to survive. many of us are scared of love but to think of love within arms length, embracing us while we cower in pain, terrified appeals our sanity. for what use are of hands, if not to hold another.

poets have written, operas have been sung, yet love's flourish is unlike any other. a force stronger than the earth's magnet, willing you towards me, perhaps? an embrace that consumes you, yet you feel infinite. i'd wish on dandelions for you, long for you... and maybe be met with the searing daggers of reality. it's not easy, to love a person beyond oneself, to lose every sense in that one person. it's not clean, it's messy, ugly, even. i'm an obscurial, you'd be my haven.

friends exist, to make you appreciate love all the way more. but hearing and reading is one thing, experiencing it is another. a fantasy so immersed in my being that watching is joyful, but somehow makes a bud of pain blosssom in my lungs. maybe they become sobs that pour out, or press under the weight of those breaths i've held, longing for you. was it too much to hope for, that you'd arrange my stars into constellations? look at them and not close your eyes to the light.

perhaps someday you'd run. someday you'd run far and fast, bare feet through the forest clumps. you'd jump over the little streams and dodge the hanging branches, believing you're running for freedom. you'd say it was freedom but deep inside you'd know freedom is just another fancy word for the lingering solitude on your neck. the realization would haunt you and you'd trip on one of the vines crawling on the ground.

you'd lay there, in measured agony with bruises on your knees and dried tears in your eyes.

you'd wait for someone to come for you, a love you never had. you'd wait for them to come around, not as a knight to pick you up, for you're completely capable of doing that yourself. you'd wait for them to lay besides you, looking at starless skies, sharing the misery and calling it love.

—Saif Madre & Eeshita Bhattacharjee

all the myths on love

i. love equates to a broken heart

aren't we all scared? to let the chaos that love is, to run within our veins, giving it power to wreck havoc on us, to rip us apart in shreds that would never conjure just right. but perhaps there will always be people that disappear, making empty promises with no intention of fulfilling, but somewhere someone would carry the bandage and love would appear as a saving grace rather than a nightmare. love doesn't hurt, loving the wrong person does.

ii. it's all sunshine and rainbows

don't mistake the last paragraph as a fact that if not painful, love is purely beautiful. for if you do, you'd be accused of being quite irrational to begin with. love is simply the grey area, granting us moments of happiness to live with. while we could totally well in the absence of it too, we yearn for it as humans tend to always look for more than they have. perhaps love is the salvation we seek, unbeknownst to the fact that it is capable of stirring up more chaos than we could imagine.

iii. it is too cheesy to digest

we, as a generation, has taken it upon ourselves to divide people in boxes and categories, while simultaneously shifting ourselves from the apex position to those lower than hell. and somewhere between lies the kind of romantics whom we believe would die in each other arms, our remarks rarely said in awe, often in disgust. lest we wash our eyes off judgement, we might see love blooming like we don't understand. and don't we taint all that not fits in the crevices of our conscience?

iv. fights leads to breakups to irrevocable tears

if you cut open your chest, you'd see your insides moving uneasily with past trauma. dig a little deeper and you'd reach old insecurities you pushed in forcibly but never thought of throwing it away. well, a spoiler; you can't. it's a part of you, nevertheless ugly and capable of pain. but what you can do, is soothe it. google would advice you to talk to your partner, and it wouldn't hurt you for once to listen if you don't wish to cry sleepless nights later. maybe try with slacking off the edges of your ego and you might find solutions your reckless soul never tried to look for.

v. always and forever

oh the inherent romanticism of always and forever! haven't we read those words every now and then? on the corners of poetries and the promises they made to you. but it's all a lie. not that love does not exist, but if you think logically, people die and so does their love exception being someone someday might take you as their muse only if you're lucky enough. and all that's immortal is written to be tragic, the pain resonating with hearts erupting with desires to relive it. perhaps forever is not what we should seek, but present is all that should suffice our heart and soul. for mortality is a present that we misunderstood and all that ends, is only what stands to be true.

—Saif Madre

afterlife perhaps?

do you know? grief magnifies in silence. the melancholy within us echoes to the horizon and back and our heart pounds inside a wooden ribcage, attempting to escape the confinement forced upon it. you think of so many tomorrow's but your sanity is still stuck in the graveyards of past. your crooked nails hurt your skin until the blood turns cold and your humanity withers like the petals of a rose left uncared for.

you float out of the grave dug for your last rites, but you seem to lack the body that you seem to have occupied for the years you were said to be alive. your name is scribbled on the tombstone in chalk outlines and love from those you knew and vice versa showcased in the form of the most beautiful of plucked flowers from a nearby garden. and it comes to light, of the smell that woke you up from the beauty sleep scheduled till eternity.

is it fun? the disappearance from the human world as some weep for you to come back and some while indifferent to your absence, use it as an excuse to dodge assignments as they supposedly moan in your remembrance.

you finally understand what lies on the other side of the blackhole, the other dimension where no mortal soul could reach without sacrificing what's most dear to them; their life.

you were afraid of the shadows when you were a kid. when the shadows grew bigger, your innocent heart saw them as monsters that would gulp you down. your parents used your fears as a bait, making you eat the broccoli or the shadow would possess you and how it never likes bad kids. so you tried to be good.

you tried to be better rather. you tried so much that you ended up destroying yourself. and now, you're the shadow. you would watch as you're used as the reason to force perfection in naive souls. you would see the cycle operating and how snapped strings of dreams are thrown into the same realm as yours, just because they were afraid to step out of line.

you stand outside the window of your family house. it's been a long time since your body was found in the ditch. the tears have dried and the memories of you seem to be long forgotten. your father has a smile as he stands proud at your sister's achievements. you realize that in life if agony is inevitable, so is happiness. you are happy that they have found closure, but it pains your dead heart that they forgot you so soon.

but you don't come back when the night falls. for that's when your absence is vibrant in the house. you don't see your father staring into space, longing to hear your voice. your sister sleeps in your clothes so as to feel you're close to her, holding her like you did once.

your mother still makes you tea at midnight and cries as she washes the cup. your best friend writes letters to you and burns them for you would never read them now. this is the language of the grievers. they mourn in silence until their heart squeezes by the pain of your absence.

you go back again, in the cold grave. you know you have to move forward from the earthly miseries, but nobody likes to move on. it is hard not to see their faces again, but what choice do you have. it pains more to see their faces and not touch them. so you lay again, confident that you're ready to whatever is destined in your fate. the soft touch of the heaven, or the brunt of hell. you sleep, and leave it to the gods to choose if you would live the life of a ghost again or would witness the afterlife perhaps?

—Saif Madre

Is it still called love?

Is it still called love when it's painful?
The ankles locking trips you
To fates you would have never dreamt of
The heavy heart capable of breaking
All the bones in your weary ribcage and
Humming a rhythm of pain
Is it still called love if it breaks your heart?

Is it still called love when it's too unfamiliar?
Too different to comprehend
Too difficult to live with
When your mind seems to be wrapped
In a wrong box of emotions
And you can't help but question it
Is it still called love if it's never steady?

Is it still called love when you're understanding too much
As being left alone repeatedly

Becomes a natural habit
And toxicity appears like a home
Where everything seems to be solved
By a facade of rewritten apologies
Is it still called love or compromise?

Is it still called love when it reeks of lies?
When the spring falters
And all the promises withers
Under the shadow of truth
All the belief you harbored
Is wrecked amidst the chaos
Is it still called love if it's devoid of trust?

Is it still called love if it feels unreal?
All the reality seems like an illusion
Thrusted in your subconscious
As you lay disoriented from the reality
And when fiction creeps to your neck
Making you doubt your existence
Is it love? Or a hallucination

Is it still called love when it suffocates you
The poison in their words
Takes effects slowly on your mind

Twisting it in ways oblivious to sanity
And all the sweet words nourish hatred
In deep corners of heart with innocence lost
Is it still called love when it's killing you?

—**Saif Madre**

what intimacy really means

i. holding hands

have you ever thought? what could be more divine in this world of separate individuals than intertwined fingers. because we hold someone's hand, maybe we give us a part of us to them in the name of love. we let them guide us through tough times and cheerful days, we let them twist our fate, and it's just the inherent belief we behold that what we end up is beautiful, that they will lead us to the twilight where dawn and dusk part ways and ours is conjured.

ii. eye contact

imagine you're only a minute away from dying, wouldn't you wish to drown yourself in their hazel irises, irrespective of how moist it is. there is also something so pretty in the meeting of eyes, the realization that while world is looking for stars in the sky, you have found your universe in their big, innocent eyes crazed with some scheme you might regret sometime later. and one blink of their eyes would tell you how love is all but steady.

iii. inside jokes and shared grins

smiles are contagious, they spread to all of whom you love sans any pretence. and someday while conversing, some words make you look at them, capable of bringing a stretch even on your tear stained face. may it be a snippet about a hometown cafe, or an excerpt from a novel you never gave them back, some words as you know, belong to just to the two of you, translating the polka dot dreams you weaved a weekend night wishing for the day you're living today.

iv. forehead kisses

what are imprints? those parts you mark on them, not terrorizing but calling a place in where you can return. scars that don't pain with longing, where unmade promises are committed upon because sometimes words fall short. so when you kiss their forehead out of all affection the world could give to a person, their love on your lips leaves a mark, one reeking of such warmth that you'd never forget because how can someone forget the path they paved to their home.

v. sacrifices and stars

sacrifices. they're hard, to not choose something you like, but sometimes the sacrifices, they're worth the happiness you grant someone. and may it be something as trivial as waking early to meet them, or to stay behind for them when the party is in the other room, or to dancing to the beats of their heart but it's still a language of love, pure as ever. so maybe someday when you're set for netflix and chill, and they ask you "would you like to stargaze with me?" do not hesitate to nod like crazy and shut the laptop, because sometimes love is finding your happiness in those of others.

vi. staying nevertheless

easy isn't something destiny is fond of. dilemmas are what you dodge on a monday evening until someday you both get hurt. there might be arguements, disagreements and such. standing in a multitude of peace is what we all desire but isn't peace a hoax we all run after. an illusion we made up for chaos persists despite all. but maybe when all is spoken, your love for them would never be compromised. still unheard prayers would be made, secretly smiling at you, and still the breezes would whisper their name to you. for love is what we all do, but it only comes down to "if we could stay in love?"

—Saif Madre

To the one I couldn't bring myself to love

How would you start a letter asking for apologies? Because I am quite ill equipped with the normal acts of humanity, and now that I don't have you to push me over cliffs, I feel helpless. And maybe, I don't understand your pain of not being the one, but I wish you'd know that the one being left behind isn't a relief either.

If I knew you'd fall in love with me, I would've been ready. I would've let you walk into my holiday house of horrors, let you rip open the curtains, so that you could peek a glance at my vulnerabilities, I would've saved your drowning heart with my name inscribed on it. If I knew beforehand, that you would fall for me, I would've caught you before it was too late.

Would you happen to know, how after some moments of reveal, fragments of your past, dance before your eyes, finally making you realise the series of event? For now I remember, how you'd know melancholy was my favourite song, how sometimes I would watch a glint in your eyes while you looked at me, how you'd write of sweet nothings about someone, who you'd deny to reveal. Maybe you can be what the stars warned me about, a love so forbidden.

What justice would I do to you, if I give you my broken heart? One under burden of such earthly miseries that my sanity creeps out of its crevices, and a soul crushed beyond repair by a summer fling, that flung me out of shape to be capable of love. And we are separate beings, being held together by a string, a bridge I can't cross because I'm too afraid of falling, not for you, but from my sanity.

As comforting as fiction is, at the end of the day, it's just a synonym for unreal. Only if our lives were made of "I love you, you love me; a perfect love story," I would've told you how I have longed for your presence, skipping red lights, ignoring red flags for you. But how can I give you my everything, when I am empty too? How can I love, when I don't believe in it?

Believe me when I say, I wish my heart wanted you. That my soul had melted on the unconditional love that you showered upon me, that the album of memories pushed me into a nostalgia of you and me. For you were what I was searching for, until all I was left to find was me and my scattered love. So maybe our love wasn't cursed, the timing was.

And thank you for not going quietly. But to stomp down towards the alley, screaming of my wickedness, pushing me away. If it had made you feel better, I'd let you slap me. For silence would be a torture for me, twisting me in ways I could never fathom. But leaving you took my soul as a souvenir, imprinting a wretched fate for me, as my bleeding guilt tells me I deserve.

And just so you know, I never said goodbye to you. For you belong to my heart and soul, romantically or not.

—Saif Madre

Other pov:

To the one I still love

I received your letter of apologies, if one could call it that. And this is the third draft I am writing, slashing out rude remarks and taunts I have been holding back. But keeping aside the denial I've been drowning in, I would want you to know that you've nothing to apologise for. Love is strange, and people aren't homes and it's a load of crap for all we know. And it's not people to be blamed for, but mere expectations of them.

To all the times you mentioned I shouldn't have left, I didn't know where else to go. For I knew all my sentences would just be words stringed together when I'd hear you speak, for the idea of me without you seemed hazardous and to think about anyone like that scared me, for to see a single glimpse of you and not fall in love all over again wasn't an easy gamble for me and I'd have enough of scraped knees for a lifetime.

If you look out your window, at the broken window of my old house, you would remember of the fight I had with my mother, that I confided in you. What you didn't know was when you hugged me and told me

I was like a sibling to you, that fuelled the following consequences concluding with the broken window. So maybe you'd realize now that all I did was save you from me, for while you believe I deserve better, maybe you deserve the best.

I have nightmares about us. Sometimes I wake up, sometimes I deny to. They end the same way, you fading into nothingness as we step forward to kiss and I sit there in absolute loneliness, reliving something that I never lived and I would never fathom the difference between the living and the hallucinations for all it is, is a hell loop for me. And now all I've deduced is what I believed to be a heart full of love was just a mispronunciation for hurt full of love.

I am now aware of the fact that I have always liked to run. Run away from dilemmas I can't face, hide from confrontations, block my mind from the thoughts of "if i could ever be more for you?" And fhe worst to leave you so to absolve myself of the sin of loving you, to feel emotions that I vowed to be foreign to. But maybe I was mistaken, for leaving you made me love you more and to think that if distance does make my heart grow fonder, if you were mine to keep, I would've loved you to superlative

And thank you. Thank you for letting me go when I tugged the hand you held for stopping me. For if you would've stopped me, asked me to stay once more, I would've complied, nonetheless let the decision destroy me. And maybe we weren't meant to be, I know, rich coming out of me, but maybe it really wasn't our time. Maybe the fates preferred the cruelty of reality over comfort of the fictional love I had for you. But if we have better luck another time, say, will you meet me in another life?

—Saif Madre

Remember me, won't you?

When the sound of raindrops
Fall on your ears as a melody
And the storm outside your porch
Brews emotions floating over surreal words
When you wake up at twilight
To find the serene rainbow before your eyes
Remember me, won't you?

When you're drunk in poetry
One that I wrote you
And you sleep with a diary aside
With my handwriting scrawled on the pages
When the story ends with a tragic ending
That I once recited to you
Remember me, won't you?

When you spend the summer
In your grandmother's house
And lifeless blossoms of flowers
By the running creek amuses you

When the beauty of their midnight gospels
Keeps you up every night
Remember me, won't you?

When your tongue craves nectarine
Plucked straight from the trees
And your heart longs for happiness
One not filtered by sorrow and pain
When the stars and tsunamis in your eyes
Bleeds of an impending infinity
Remember me, won't you?

When the roses in your gardens wither
And lilacs bleed mauve
When the footprints on the mud
Is shoveled and forgotten
When your saffron skin is healed
By the wounds that thorns inflicted
Remember me, won't you?

I saw you today
By your old childhood home
You looked happy and naive
Oblivious of my presence
And you seemed to have forgotten
About the promise you made me when I asked
Remember me, won't you?

Tangerines on my dinner table

the tangerines on my dining table
taste a lot like you; bittersweet
and my mom has noticed
how i have been peeling more of them
since the last time we met.
every time your hands brushed against mine
my heart fluttered out to you
and everytime you recited to me
the sappy love poems you wrote
the world felt more just,
the sins answerable
for didn't everybody say?
everything is fair in love and war.
your name however sounds
like a long lost memory
but i still remember the syllables
every morning i wake up
my friend tells me to get over you
and i want to say i try

but it would be a white lie
for our fates are interwoven in ways
even universe could never separate.

—**Saif Madre**

a catastrophic love

we were both made of catastrophes
burning; stricken with grief
it was hard that we both stayed
but would be if you'd ever leave.
i stroke your hair slowly
as if caressing a tender sadness
could feel the tremors of us breaking
but only if it would make me love you less.
we hold hands in the brackish winter
i see imprints of my ring on your finger
when was it that you stopped wearing it?
forgetting you vowed to have it forever.
was our love compromised?
or was it a case of vanity and hubris?
we have come a long way now
but being loved by you is something i dearly miss.
nevertheless, i am trying to make the most of it
picking pieces of us we recklessly threw
for the world would be collapsing
I'd never stop loving you.

—**Saif Madre**

loving you was like

i. loving you was like a hard gamble, one against the odds of the fate and destinies written of the stars. it was a gamble i took, shamelessly and recklessly for you. loving you was worth the chance of falling in love with you, for your eyelashes held more wishes aligning our fates than a preacher would predict.
ii. loving you was like an open book, one you handed me before thinking twice. it was trust and loyalty intertwined in our hands, compassion in your eyes and a sense of belonging when you had kissed me. loving was the unwavering truth and a promise to be kept, an oath when I'd tell you, "you know me better than i do myself."

iii. loving you was an unkempt garden, one where the weeds are nurtured not slacked. weeds are very common, and unwillingly frustrating, but weeds aren't a reason to abandon a garden. just as loving you was telling you of your flaws, not snatching them off your hands. loving you was the inherent act of observation, if you had try to improve for my sake, for our sake.

iv. loving you was like violence, but the silent kind. it was how I'd uproot the world if it was unjust to you. it was to acknowledge your undying worth and absolving any sins that had dare to touch even the tiniest of a strand of your hair. loving you was a lingering kiss on the forehead, believing it had ward off any evil lurking in the corner, for love is the greatest religion i am aware of.

v. loving you was like remembering, every part of you. it was the insoluble memory of everything that is tied to your existence, the scars that you hold dearly, the dimple by your chin, the letter your brother wrote for you before he left overseas. loving you was forgetting for a moment, what not remembering you felt like.

vi. loving you was like coming back home, not a place but a person. it was the comfortable silences where we read and narrate our favourite stanzas to each other. it was the hanging confessions that are better communicated unsaid. it was the flickering of eyes, a partaking longing to embrace them in a "break-a-rib" sort of hug. loving you was knowing there would always be you to return to at the end of the day.

—Saif Madre

are you still there?

"are you still there?" i knock on your door and nobody answers, as a part of me already knew but didn't want to accept. how could i accept that you are just not there anymore when once you always were. you made me grow into you, you became a habit, one that isn't particularly easy to let go. because i am trying to erase the traces of you, the sound of your laugh, your oddly affectionate sarcasm from my mind and all it does is remind me of you more.

it has been 365 days of grief, clear and distinguished grief now since the day they buried you down the grave, and i stood there waiting like a forlorn kite, one abandoned at collapsed terraces. waiting that you'd jump out, scream how it's just another of your practical jokes and I'd punch you hard for making me cry. but you really like to keep me waiting because it's a year now and my fists miss the feeling of spurting blood from your crooked nose.

do you remember the burning building we saw as toddlers? the fire trucks, the corpse of a fireman who died saving an old woman. you said how pathetic it was of him to give up his good life for one that was already close to mortality. i told you of how he was a martyr and how his family must be proud of him. something you said then really stuck with me still, for i have not yet forgotten the sound of you saying, "what good is pride when there is larger grief to suffer from."

pity looks are the worst. there, i said it. there are a lot of ways to console somebody left behind, starting with normalcy if you must? but the world strives on sympathy, give and take of it. they would stare at you as if grief has blinded you from grief, they would whisper your name, as if the unheard cries aren't enough torture. you were a part of me that has ceased to exist suddenly, and i am not sure if i could cope with it without you, ironic when it's your very absence that has caused it.

it is funny how we can't express love but our obituaries lasts till bleeding ears. for i am aware i never really told you the amount of gratitude that my sanity upheld for you. i want to tell you, really but the void, the emptiness has drained out any words, maybe because agony doesn't have a language or perhaps something told me words didn't communicate as much emotions among us as certain vibes did.

i wonder if you're enjoying the afterlife in hell or is it your translucent ghost that has been staring at me from across the hall. a quick reminder, life too has been a living grave if it provides any sadistic pleasure to you. the memories of ghost town have done an explicit job of haunting me of your presence. i see you everywhere and do not mistake it for an obsession but perhaps a brotherly love very few could hang of. my words sound like i am in denial, waiting frantically for you to come back soon, but i am perfectly oka...wait i hear something. is it you? was it you?

are you still there?

—Saif Madre

running from my demons

i run away. fast, faster
than my demons on the other side
it seems like a forever
the gaping wounds they left too wide.
but they always catch up on me
trip me by my leg on the asphalt of the road
i crawl away with a bleeding knee
and a bruised vulnerability little too exposed.
a frostbite ache numbs my head
and regret infest my heart
i wish i would end up dead
a pinnacle of a destroyed art.
it doesn't take long to know
my shadows are the demons
capable of a death too slow
as if sinning is their only religion.
there is a storm in my chest
and a hurricane in my eyes
but i cannot tell anyone lest

they'd see my agonizing cries.
there is light oh hope at the end
but i'm afraid i'd perish before
as i am tired to even pretend
that my hands could reach the oars.
i am falling apart and no one knows
for i don't know how to tell them
that i need to be saved, i suppose
before the demon again chants my name.

—**Saif Madre**

saying forever too soon

the peace in this room
is too stagnant to breathe in
so i scrape the walls off
screaming of all my sins
perhaps the gods would forgive me
for all that i did wrong
or perhaps the suffering is eternal
one that was already too prolonged.
it is now everyday
that i trip on your white picket fence
catching a glimpse of you
out of words to explain a love a little too immense
for i have lost you in myself
and all that's keeping me sane
is your promise you'd return
but what good is love if it's for vain.
so can i make you my home again?
so under the starry skies and a crescent moon
i'd let you ruin me slowly with a love like that
holding hands and saying forever too soon.

A kiss under the misletoe

A kiss under the misletoe
A hundred vows exchanged
Was our story worth the time?
Or another love ending in vain?
Angels swaying below the hearth
Devil horns poking out the fireplace
Would you leave me when the night ends?
Or agree nonchalantly if i ask you to stay?
Stars forged out of indigo
A moon too heavy for the sky
Will you wait for me till my words align?
Or does forever seems too much of a lie?
Mascara smudged eyes
Trembling hands; lips to pursue
Can you answer me honestly?
When I whisper a rushed i love you.

—Saif Madre

Tackling An Apocalypse a short story

it's been a long time. the worlds have collided, the stars are on the ground, zombies have replaced humanity as the apex predators while all that's left of humanity is shreds and pieces hiding in underground bunkers, waiting to be devoured by the undead. we have been looking for a cure to rise again but there are already people by a fist or two to sustain any collateral damage.

while we hid in the bunkers, the zombies evolved. while we cried ourselves to sleep, blaming the gods, the zombies became more deadly. they sniffed out the smelliest of us and as a necessity we had to bid those whose feet made us hold our breaths. some redeemed, some did not. some readily sacrificed themselves for the greater good, some were thrown out. after all, pity always comes after survival.

many relatives were lost, many separated. sins were repented and new one's made. we were on the brink of losing, actually no, we already did lose. now we were counting down till the horrendous urge of hunger would gobble us down before the zombies did. it didn't matter to me till my younger brother was with me, nothing mattered till his limbs were attached to his body, till his breathing had that rhythm, till his eyes scrunched up every time he laughed. life turned tragic to him earlier than it was just, when mom and dad died, or to say it in a un-mild manner, when mom and dad were eaten alive as if the last french fry on a plate for three.

that day he didn't say anything, neither cried, nor complained of the unduly nightmares that haunted him till he was awake. but he pretended as if nothing was wrong, and i pretended with him for that's what I've always done. he made friends with the rats that gutted up from the sewers but the friendship was always shortlived for anything smelly deserved to die, as per the new unmade democratic laws by those of us who were left. but only if we knew that there was one friend he hid from us with the scent of fragnant roses. but only if the disguise fooled the predators waiting to sink their teeth in us.

it wasn't long before the zombies followed us to our hideout. most probably it was just us 7 left to survive, and we were oblivious to the storm at our doorstep(or to be precise, the large iron safe doors that guarded whatever life was left in us). it was a regular monday morning for us except we never really could

distinguish between day and night anymore. the sun did feel far now because all our cold bodies longed for, was a bit of sunlight. but hell broke loose when the grunting of the lifeless corpses thumping on the grounds above disrupted our morning(or evening) breakfast. i wondered if satan had visited us personally to dip us in the shallow waters of agony. or whether it was just the zombies, just the neighbourhood, not-so-friendly zombies.

we packed up our bags and i hugged my brother, maybe it was our last hug or maybe i am over-dramatic. there wasn't much of a competition for us and even it comes to worst, i doubt dear aunt Rosetta's sewing needles would do as much damage. the thumping grew louder and we got prepared, to fight or to die was a question undeserving of an answer. cursing the gods didn't do much good when the iron doors was slaughtered but they crossed the limits when it was my brother they went for. as an act of retaliation or pure foolishness, i bit the zombie's hand before he could bite the devilish angel i had for a brother. and then we realized, hope isn't as rogue as we make it to be.

the zombie skin disintegrated and came out a human, in tattered jeans and a tank top. maybe karma was at play or maybe the god of luck blessed my jaws. whatever it be, we all shared a knowing look and then frenzy was the only word that reminds me of what actually happened. everyone started biting everyone, and before the zombies could retreat there were more humans than them. the numbers game always works.

i was disappointed how my parents couldn't be bitten back to not being devoured by the zombies but at least we knew a way to retaliate now. my brother was safe and as i mentioned before, nothing mattered as long as i had him besides me.

—Saif Madre

all the tender words you said to me

"you look like moon in a satin dress"

it was long ago that i had smiled wide, careless before today. it always took great efforts to feel good about myself before i met you. i was always the silent, shy kind until you came along and now chaos prevails in my mind. so when you look at me and tell me about the beauty you see in my eyes, i believe it. i believe you for your face would betray the love you hold for me even if you never say it outright.

"this reminded me of you"

you text me bits of love by writers renowned for their fables and tell me how you want it all with me, just not in fiction. everytime you take my name, my insides churn in anticipation of you, for to believe you know me, remember me even in my absence feels to good to be real. you whisper to me, "if i was a supervillain, faced by a choice to choose you or a conspiracy, i wouldn't think twice before taking you with me, for you are the sin even god would forgive me for." and i look at you, helpless, so helpless in love.

"you mean the world to me"
the mere words could feel as if an over exaggeration, a writer's play with the wonders of words. but when you tell me this, i see how your eyes scrunch up tight, how your smile creases at right angles. i see how no other honest man could compete with the truthfulness in your voice. you clasp our hands together and i feel the warmth of universe beneath our fingers, one you kept apart for me, for eternity seems bearable with you.

"daisies bloom at the sight of you"
oh, do you remember that day when the destiny held beef against me and it felt easy to fall apart then keep holding the strings putting me together? do you remember the grin on your face as i never seemed to stop ranting at minor inconveniences in my life? i had hit you for laughing at me but couldn't resist giving in to the laugh either. i asked whether you thought if i was a bad person, and you told me that while it was evil of me to take your share of pizza slice, i was otherwise the sunshine that brightened your day, the art that never let your life go bland.

"i would choose you in every lifetime"

promises often seem debatable to me, the idea of a said forever torn at seams, the i love you's a little bitter at the end. but with you, i have seen how you have lived upto what you say, how your actions weigh more than any promise to be made. your lips pour reassurance on the burns of my insecurities with no hesitation at all. so let it be love in slow motion or flaws crippling us apart, i seem to have found a home in you, one i'd inhabit with no regrets whatsoever.

—Saif Madre

"i want to narrate you a story."

"i want to narrate you a story."

i wonder if it was the scorching sun making us pant and huff or the fact that the class we bunked would cost us an hour of writing assignments. but when she called me, it was impossible to resist, i said yes in an instance afraid that second thoughts would make her take the offer back. she took me through a daffodil field and i was mesmerised how the sun shone through her dandelion eyes and hazel strands of hair.

we slowly made our way to an abandoned funfair with a perfectly working ferris wheel. apparently she made friends with a now vagabond who once ran this funfair. she took me up to a ferris wheel and made it stop.

"do you want to hear the story or not?" she asked when i didn't say anything.

"i- i am afraid of heights." i managed to utter.

"look in my eyes." she whispered and i did.

i looked at those orbs of fire that were capable of burning the gods to bones, i saw her rose tinted cheeks and how they scrunched up when she smiled. i looked at her delicate hands that would either caress your face or choke you to a merciless death.

"yes, tell me."

"a girl liked a boy and so did he like her back. but the mutual attraction was never spoken off, the hands brushing against each other and stolen glances were a forbidden to talk of. she never realized when it evolved to love, when he became more important than any living soul to occupy the heart. but she never told him. why would she? she was the girl, it was the guy's responsibility no matter how naive and shy he must be. so they both held their silence. and they still do."

"that was an amazing sto-"

"i don't want to be my mother. i can't wait for you to speak your damn mouth out till you're sure of me. so, yes we have been best friends for long, but i wouldn't settle for less if you're the one i want. for you bring me comfort even in sadness, for when i call your name, the syllables of your name lingers like sweet cherries in my mouth. i love you and I wouldn't bargain what i feel for you with anything in the world." she spoke out in rushed words but every letter rung through my ears and jumbled through my nervous mind."

"i think i want to kiss you." i said, flabbergasted at her words and even at my own but with a hint of pride too.

"think less, kiss more." she said and pushed her lips against mine and i felt the taste of heaven enamour my mortal body. you looked at me when you pulled back, and asked me leaning closer, “do you fear the heights yet?”

and i said, “only if you aren’t holding my hands.”

in sometime, we were off the ferris wheel, walking out of abandoned funfair when i asked her,

“was it your mother you were talking about? in the story?”

“yes. the stereotypes made her a silent lover.”

“who was the guy she loved?

“someone in her college. he became a big name in this town for sometime but soon forgot him. now he is as poor as one could be scrapping off old meals.” she waved at the vagabond with a wide grin and asked me

“so did you like my could-have-been father?”

falling out of love

one fine day, another of our grumbly visits to grocery stores, you asked me what did falling out of love felt like. i told you of the silent heartbreak and uncomfortable silences. how once entangled strands, separate as if an act of god. you asked me how to know, and i said to detect if it's love or guilt they hand you. i asked if it was our fate, and you promised me how you were always waiting for me at the sunrise and how falling out of love wasn't your thing

but suddenly there was a sudden coldness in your embrace, it felt you were slipping away and if i held you tight, you'd break and i promised never to break you. your lips tasted of poison and there was a hesitation when you said your i love you's. your eyes don't find me in a crowd anymore and the forehead kisses feel compromised now. and all that ran through my mind was if you were starting to fall out of love.

when i wrote you a poem, a sonnet to glorify your muse, you told me how it was just nice. i remember telling you how art is a confession of my undying love for you and you told me immortality is cursed. when i brought you flowers, you gave them to someone else, and when i asked you told me they'd wilt under your eyes, like i did. i cried sleeping that night, wondering if this is what falling out of love is like for you?

i asked you that day, when you cried but never showed, to lay your scars out in rows for me and you said you scrape them before anyone could see. when i kissed you and you asked me to stop, i did. when i asked why, you told me that there was too much of love in it and too much of something is hazardous. so i reminded myself to love you in bits and pieces. but even that was too much for you, since you asked me that question. maybe you already fell out of love already.

and when i, with a heavy heart went to ask you of it, of the undying love that was dead now and the muse that was torn to shreds by the thorns you casually called honesty, you planted your lips on mine in a reckless manner, till the poison felt like honey again and all your eyes shined of was my reflection. you asked for forgiveness for you were trying to see i would stay for you as i vowed i would. i still wonder what hell would break loose if i told you the truth before you said anything, if i told you I'd fallen out of love.

—**Saif Madre**

and we compare

and we compare
when we run out of arguments
when the grief is too heavy
to be justified in excuses.
we compare when the longing is everlasting
the longing for the greener grass
when the better appears so lustrous
that the good appears as worst.
we compare when we want more
and more, and more
till our hollow selves are filled
with reassurance and promises.
we compare for that's what we have known
we compare because if we don't,
we'd end up in vain.

—Saif Madre

what of those?

what of those
who die too soon?
an excuse for their absence
their residence among stars and moon.
what of their weak memories
their name a slight bluff
who is said to love us most
but their love never being enough.
what of the i love you's gone astray
a hiccup at their mention
all wary blurred thoughts
a living ghost worthy of attention.
what of the photos burned at edges
poetries sung in tragedies
a heart too cold for a familiar touch
a soul never less fascinated by mortality.

—Saif Madre

never Never Never

and i wonder every other day
what would change in the world
if i left with no prior notice
for i am aware the sun would still shine
nor would the moon be less bright
would the stars fall on earth
if i dared to be one of them
out of this world
lesser in agony; more in freedom.
as the tears are brimming
on the very edge of my iris
murky waters clog my throat
and wisdom held tightly on my tongue
for truth is acknowledged bitter
if it's against you.
i have dreamed of a many better things
on the other side of the door
but they push me aside
whisper in my burnt ears

that it is sinful of me
to linger where i shouldn't
albeit my barbed wire body
has more scars than joints
cigarette butts the only warmth
on my cold lifeless being.
it is wiser to check twice
if the rope is tight enough
or all you're left with
is a strangled throat
and threats to wring it apart
as if i didn't try enough
as if i failed again
and i hear them laughing at me
"never good enough" they say
and it echoes
never never never.

—**Saif Madre**

A quick guide on loving a sociopath

i. Take a knife. Not a blunt one, like their emotions, one with a sharp edge and carve your insides. Serve your one heart, thousand feelings to them on a silver platter and watch as they throw it all down the drain.

ii. Are you injured with invisible scars? Reopened scars that bleed more profusely? One that does not stay covered by the bandages of the words of those who really care about you? Then, I must congratulate you, you're making progress.

iii. Window shopping is what you should love and envy the most. You go around, looking at expressive partners, hearing words of affection that never fell on your love deprived ears. You imagine what it must be like, to love and be loved, but you come out of the imagination, for reality is as miserable as it could get

iv. If love could talk, it would tell you how it longs to reach out to you, but is always held back by jealousy, accusations and such. And you are used to them, you do not see love without it's withdrawals. You do not see a love not tainted.

v. You're a wildflower, growing against the odds. Them, the gardener who once recognized you for your beauty, praising you like none ever did.

But while you wish to lay your petals on them, you realize they're here to make love to the violets.

vi. You find yourself weilding blades, wishing to harm yourself, because physical pain seems less tortuous than the silent chaos wreaking havoc on your mind. Your stomach hurts from throwing up poison glazed in honey. They look up at you, ask what's wrong. You say you're okay. And you die within yourself again.

vii. Have you ever wondered? What's more toxic? A knife to your throat or a kiss to your lips? For a knife, it would kill you with just a sudden urge of pain but the kisses? They suck a part of you everytime they hold you against the wall against your will. You die a little when your words are termed insignificant by the brushing of those not so tender lips against yours.

viii. Look back at your life and tell me what do you see? What do you see except pain and agony? They're your world, as you say, and it's a lie you tell yourself when someone asks you why do you choose to suffer. Tell me, are you in love or are you in denial?

A quick guide on being a sociopath

i. Take a large blanket. Not a pure one, like their souls, one stinking of carelessness and immaturity like you. Wrap your astray emotions in them, and lock it away for an eternity. For all you've known is that vulnerability makes you weak.

ii. Did you manage to hurt them? Carve their skin with your nagging apathy? Unload heaps of insecurities deep in their bones? Throw the curse dagger you yield, reeking of rage straight on the bullseye, their heart? Then I must congratulate you, you're making progress.

iii. When they look at you, with expectations of expressions of love brimming in their eyes, look away. Don't look back at their innocent requests of showing love, for to love, is to destroy. And you're just an ordinary person with a hand me down heart, one incapable of affection and such.

iv. If you ever lean against them, you could hear satin lullabies etched into their velvet hearts. But pull away before the soft humming sounds manipulates you to open knots of the rusty layers tied by the chain of miseries. Pull away before they can see how empty you're, how your rigid body lacks a soul.

v. Stroll up to a garden with them, at the crack of dawn, and tell them how they're the wildflower, beautiful in their own mysterious ways. And then pick out all the violets one by one, so they know only they deserve to be in the garden. But have they run away? Did they misinterpret, that you would choose others before you? It's okay, misunderstandings is a language of love.

vi. When they tell you, that they're okay, while their face recites a different story. Will you believe them and let them be? Or try to listen to them rant about how wicked of a person you're? Would you walk with them, on the bridge of bandages, covering every blister you inflicted? Or walk away, trusting their word, no matter if it sounds like a cry of attention?

And before you know, they've disappeared into thin air.

vii. When they finally confront you, on you being distant, do you answer? Do you apologise, or hyacinths bloom in every crevice of your throat? You nod and listen to them let everything out, wishing you could do the same. But you just tell them, that you inflicted pain on them because there was too much of it inside you. And don't they say? Sharing is caring.

viii. And when all is over, you apologise to them and they listen to you like they always have, you make promises to change, promises you don't know, you'll deliver on, or will it be the delivery of heartbreak that ceases your hesitation to commit. When the story ends, depicting a forever you could only dream of, tell me, are you being loved or pitied on?

—**Saif Madre**

What did my grief look like?

My therapist asked me today
What did my grief look like?
And I sat idly to wonder
What is it that haunts me
Everyday everytime
Where all my flaws seem vibrant
And me, a dart board for it's agony

Is it my mother's corpse?
In a graveyard with no tombstones
I call her name and there is nothing
Nothing but a loud silence
But it is understandable by her part
For would you answer to someone
Whose voice you never heard?

Is it the best friend?
Who got tired of me
And my endless trauma
That leaks off me
In blood and painful words

So much that he never called back
And I still wait for him to do so

Is it the bunch of funny guys?
Who don't know humour
If it's not inflicted on me
And my helplessness
As my lips are sewn shut
When I try to protest and get instead
"Learn to take a joke."

Is it the love I never got back
While I punctured my heart
And the jagged arteries
To give more and more out
Until I fell short of it
For they asked me to be selfless
But never told me when to stop

I visited my therapist again on Monday
Where she asked if I found my grief
So I drew her a black hole with crayons
Messed around the edges
And told her that's how it looked like
Empty and dark, screaming agony
Agony that lies within me.

—**Saif Madre**

a bathroom duet

it started out as a slow hum. a reverberating sound from across the wall while i showered in my casual agony. his voice was soft, tender on the eardrums, not bearing the burden of unnecessary masculine ego that has burst my ear drums on numerous occasions. he sang couplets and i memorized the words as the melodies reached to me. i am a bathroom singer too, but my insecurities didn't let me make him the witness of my hoarse voice.

a little spying does one no bad. it didn't take long for me to figure out he was new. and it took great self control on my part to resist the urge to greet my new neighbour. the only angle i could see of him, or hear to be accurate was confined between those holy walls that once i hated. "but hatred is still an attachment" i try to convince myself.

i think i am someone who falls too fast, for in days i had fallen for him heads over heels, literally if i mention. it earned me a bump on my head but love is worth anything right? or so i heard from the novels on my shelf. i began to dream of him, or worse daydream of my mystery faceless love interest. it was just a dream, but why does it seem so real? fate favoured us, for we always matched our timings with no prior notice whatsoever. was it a sign? or just mere luck i deserved?

one day, racking up my nerves, i completed his lines. i sang where he left and didn't stop while my insides pleaded me to. it was scary and risky, but i did not care. but the silence thereafter threw me off the pedestal. the prequel to our love appeared torn and in ashes. with no further desire to prick my clumsy heart, i looked to clear up and leave. the thin walls now seemed like a curse, guilty of breaking my heart. as i was to leave, he picked up from where i left and my heart did somersaults and my grin translated my sense of euphoria. and then, we never talked in words but always in verses.

until someday he stopped suddenly. the stanzas remained blank, the lyrics incomplete. i felt incomplete. some of my friends told me how it was a pity, some astonished how someone i didn't knew could cause me such pain. i assumed he found a girlfriend and i was left alone. i waited for him but he was already gone. i told myself, life's not like the movies and i should move on from him. in the thick of healing, i stop listening to songs but still could find a hum or two dancing around my throat. i was used to his voice and now my ears were deprived of soft love.

13 long days of grieving days away, i heard him breath from across the another realm where he belonged. i asked, with nothing to lose, "are you there?" "yes." he said in a hoarse voice. it was different but his nonetheless. "where were you?" "i had cold. still have some of it. could not perform with a stuttering voice, could i?" "oh yes, or you might risk disappointing your fans, won't you?"

"the thought kept me up at nights, i swear." he chuckled and i laughed. we hummed again. hums followed by verses and melodies. it was long since we sang together, but it never affected our co-ordination. and so effortlessly healed my heart as fate brought back the bathroom duet yet again.

A Countdown to Us

3634 days back

"If we tried, we could be friends." I told her.

She looked up from the swing, her feet dangling beneath nearly touching the mud.

"Why would you want to be friends with me?" She asked in a naive voice.

"Why wouldn't I want to?"

"Everyone hates me. They call me a freak." She said, and her tears fell on the over grown orchids in the garden.

"I'd rather put it as, "I think you're freaking amazing."

I smiled to her. She smiled back.

We were friends now.

2541 days back

"Why did you pull my hair?" She asked, straightening the ribbons on her pigtails.

"You took my sandwich."

"I thought friends shared."

"But you could've asked me. I would've given you."

"I was hungry. Sorry." She said, her voice breaking.

"Hey, I was kidding. I just did that to annoy you. And you don't need to ask me. Silly friends do that."

"I thought we are friends."

"No, we are best friends."

I smiled. She smiled.

We were best friends now.

1598 days back

"How did the test go for you?" I asked her.

"I think I flunked." She frowned.

"They asked me about my position in my family. To describe it."

"What did you write?"

"I left it blank. I couldn't write how my dad beats my mom and how they fight everyday."

"You could've written anything."

"My mom hits me for lying. I wish I had a proper family."

"I can be your family." I said.

I smiled. She smiled.

We were family now.

913 days back

"So what about prom?" I asked her as we sat down for lunch in the canteen.

"What about it?"

"Who are you going with?"

"What is that of your concern?"

"I need to warn him right?"

"Who are you going with?"

"No one. I need to ask someone."

"Anyone in your sight?"

"Okay. Being shy is monotonous. Let me just ask you out."

"Huh? What?" She looked, but none could miss her cheeks reddening.

"I like you. And I want to date you."

"I think, I like you too."

I smiled. She smiled.

We were lovers now.

365 days back.

"You really need to go?" I asked, crying.

"Dad has shifted. There is no choice but to go."

"But what about us?"

"We will be in touch. We can do this." She said.

"Miss me idiot. Don't get a new partner there."

"I was thinking of doing just that."

"Shut up."

"Obviously, I would miss you. You're the only one for me."

"Write letters to me."

I smiled. She smiled.

We were pen pals now.

Today

I forgot her. She forgot me.

We are strangers now.

—Saif Madre

pretentious manual for when your loved ones leave

i. much needed denial

isn't it everyday now that you look out of your rusted windows, awaiting a shadow that your heart longs for? you have been pretending since Saturday, that loneliness hasn't devoured you yet, you have knocked doors for a familiar face but the disappointment on your face is evident when you find none. the growing pains numb you but they are nothing in front of the illusions your mind creates. you're oblivious as to the hope that nurtures poison but no one tells you otherwise for hell hath no fury like a broken heart.

ii. the resounding silence

you liked winters once. the breeze comforted your red cheeks, and evening around the fireplace with them was what you looked forward to. but it's a pity how situations destruct our aura of choices.

you shiver now, in the cold November, realizing the wide solitude you have been brewing yourself in. the illusions that once gave warmth are now guilty of burning your soul with grief like never before. the darkness engulfs you and happiness seems like a relative you'd avoid, because what good are moments of joy if they'd never stay.

iii. acceptance growing in your throat

who do you do it for? all the pain that knocks the wind out of you, who do you bear it for? you have heard that love is worth the pain but you never know until the pain blinds you, leaving you no choice but to accept the existence of it. you are expected to get used to absence, the months followed by their departure are now termed as grieving period, but isn't it endless? you sleep with their favourite flannel and somedays wake up in their shirt, but the pain is always there and all acceptance is, is a fancy word for pretentious sanity.

iv. all the questions

was there a correct response written in any of the hundred books you read for when someone asks "how are you coping?" would you tell them the infamous "im fine" or weep on their shoulders about the empty side of your bed. would you let bygones be bygones when the fake concern is showered on you, or would you let them know that it was now too late for them to care. and most importantly, what would you answer yourself, when your soul asks where is home? would you answer or drown in the helplessness of you?

v. reaching out for closure

when was it? when you were duly informed that the aforementioned grieving period was now close to ending and you should hereby conclude it by achieving closure? doesn't it sound like a game with deadlines for tasks? leave it to humanity to spice things up with all that they believe to be mundane. and the fun part is the closure to be found is mysterious, the punchline being, "when you know, you know." you are asked to move on, for people who cry on graves for long, are believed to end up just there soon. and what do you care? wasn't it your dream then, to reconcile with your lover in the most gruesome way possible?

vi. the hope for a afterlife

fairytales are beautiful. the prince meets the princess, the undying love, the pink skies, the poisoned apple, the glass slippers, the 'we stay together, we die together' kind of love, the....no wait, go back. just there. you always wanted the die together kind, it always felt enchanting. the inherent thought of living together and to plot your demise. because accept it, nobody likes to move on and the thought of sharing a grave now seems romantic to you. the clutters of bones tangled together, and the hope that their soul held on, waiting for you to join them. so you contemplate, a lot. and the driving insanity fools you into stabbing yourself for love, believing it's worth it(?) and now who knows if not fate, whether love pulled your strings together, or now you're just a corpse, another collateral damage for the namesake of love.

—Saif Madre

all the red flags hanging on you

//you make me want to fall in love//

love is terrible. it destroys hearts and upturns the fates. or so i believed, until you took me to the bright side of it. you showed me the rainbow that didn't end up alone, the tender beating hearts of gruesome beasts, the eyes that never fooled and the lips that didn't hide venomous fangs. you make me want to fall in love, and i am afraid i am too cruel for it.

//your love is too sharp for my paper hearts//

i had always held my heart on a sleeve, and a pen in my pocket, waiting for someone to sign me up for an eternity, but when you said you would love me forever, the unusual words never fit right to my ears. you love recklessly and my sanity hangs on a string, demolished by tremors and hollows of those who left. your love is too sharp for my paper hearts, and i am afraid loving me would give you a papercut.

//you call me your muse//

people say we are a perfect pair, an artist rubbing canvas with perfection and an irrational writer stringing words together for a living. but people say a lot of things, don't they? why would you only hear to them as per your convenience? i tell you i am a monster and you say you never liked the heroes anyway. you call me your muse and i don't how to tell you it's impossible to paint a mess.

//you hold me and i feel belonged//

i don't why my soul asks where is home and i whisper your name nonchalantly. i have never fit in before you came along and making you my habit scares me, terrifies even. trust came hard to me once and now i am ready to fall off a cliff knowing you'd catch me. you hold me and i feel belonged but the pit in my stomach still tells me i would be left stranded.

//we are so alike that our hearts are in sync//

when you tell me, "call me if you need me" how do i tell you i never stopped needing you. that i miss you the moment our eyes do not find each other. i wonder everyday, do you feel the same? the ruins in your veins when you think about me? are we aboard a sinking ship, that this obsession would be the end of us? we are so alike that our hearts are in sync, but if either stops, will it take the both of us down?

//you are too good for me//

why would you love me? the question haunts me, doesn't let me sleep. you're everyone's living daydream, and i, the outcast none remembers. when you first complimented me, i believed you are making fun of me, but the way you looked at me, it was unfamiliar. and it took me apart and conjoined my soul with yours. but still the insecurity persists, the question pounding in my mind. you are too good for me, and i am scared to tell you that. perhaps, love makes us selfish.

—Saif Madre

What poetry is?

If you ever wonder
What poetry according to poets is
Let me tell you
That it's a mystery
One meant to stay hidden
From gazing eyes and intrusive hearts
For on disclosure, it can destroy you

Poetry are the thoughts
Striving to survive in my head
But my mind is just like the last page of my notebook
Scribbled and messed up
Words and phrases tangled; struggling to release
That I spit on pages
And call surreal art

Poetry is just turbulent waves
Seeking the shore of insanity
Leaving imprints on sand of consciousness
Rising with pride and vanity
Until shoved down to nothing

As it returns back to the sea
Only difference being, the imprints never erase

Poetry is redemption
To deadliest of our sins
A belief that writing them down
Might excuse us from the purgatory
And a curse upon
Bestowed from angry fates
Upon us for merely existing

Poetry is the hollow
Between your neck and shoulder
One where you can hear
The breath of loneliness on you
And where your scars throb with pain
Laced with perfume to hide the stinking
Of misery and anguish

Poetry is everything
But beautiful and happy
Reeking of cold tragedies
And forgotten love
And when they call me a poet
I hesitate to nod
For I am, yet I am not

Breakup Day gone wrong

You know, people say there are two types of people during valentine's week; singles and committed. I guess I'm the third one because while I am committed, my valentine's week did go like I was single. And it wasn't because I was too mature for all this, I am a cheesy little fellow counting on the wishes of broken eyelashes as if they're capable of unleashing the beauty in the ugliest of situations.

The reason of this brooding Monday blues on my face in the days of red balloons was that things weren't going right. Me and her, we're perfect together, but thing's have been rocky for a while for no reason at all. Maybe that's what scary. The reason that there is no reason is giving rise to the uncertainty of the idea of us working it out.

So I decided to sort it all out before our ego gets the better of our relationship. I dial her number and wait for her to pick it up while another wave of anxiety hits me. No matter how long you know a person, there is always a fear of the conversation not going right, on speaking to someone after an era of silence. But we kept it as least awkward as possible and she called me to meet her on 21st of February. Maybe she wants to celebrate one day of valentine's week properly. Breakup day.

So we meet. And the fact that she wants to break everything up scares me but also flares me. So, to make her realize what she's going to lose, I wear her favorite blue mandarin collar shirt from my wardrobe and maybe she thought the same, because the idea of letting her go deserved second thoughts when she shook my heart in her black cardigan.

"You know, there are problems between both of us, right?" She asked and dabbed the ketchup on her face with fingers and I was hit by remembrance of things past us.

"Yes. I know. But can we fix it?"

"You think there is anything left to fix? We have been monotonous and I don't know, we fight every time, it's tiring for me." She continues while shaking her head and another flashback hits me. I tell my mind it's not a good time for nostalgia trips.

She looks at me, waiting for a answer and I look around to find something to help me fix this because I can't afford to lose this.

"Okay. We can't fix this. But can we dance for one last time? Just for old time's sake?" I ask, with the language of love to convince her, pointing towards the juke box.

She nods and I jumble with the buttons.

Play. Pause. Repeat.

Finally I settle for our song.

If we have each other.

The world's not perfect, but it's not that bad
If we got each other, and that's all we have
I will be your lover, and I'll hold your hand
You should know I'll be there for you
When the world's not perfect
When the world's not kind
If we have each other then we'll both be fine
I will be your lover, and I'll hold your hand
You should know I'll be there for you.

We hum around, dancing to the rhythms, when she asks,

"Is this your way of impressing me?"

"Are you going to be impressed?"

"We'll see." She says grinning

I turn her around and she is in my arms and we smile looking into each other's eyes, and apologize to each other without saying anything when my feet slip and we both fall on the ground. We look at each other in awkward silences and I wait for her to snap at me when she laughs suddenly and I laugh back. Then she again looks deep into my eyes and whispers with a smile,

"Ouch. I guess, I have fallen for you all over again."

—Saif Madre

If the world was ending tomorrow

i. If the world was ending tomorrow, would you let it sink that it's endgame now and how it's your last day on earth as human, to exist just for a mere 24 hours which you have a chance to make the most of it, or would you be cranky and complain how life is always unfair?

ii. If the world was ending tomorrow, would you, for once, let your guards down and be free, embrace your broken bones and bruised vulnerability so that you can feel all the emotions that will cease to exist soon or would you continue being strong with stacked up emotions in a suffocating heart?

iii. If the world was ending tomorrow, would you open the boxes of nostalgia with cheery memories of paper boats in the rain and wrappers of chocolates you saved for long or would you lay crying, holding the sweater of the one you left, beholding a past not worth of remembering?

iv. If the world was ending tomorrow would you give into your sweet tooth and devour the pastries from the bakery across the town and the donuts you bought for the special someone or would you continue the perfect shape, hoping god would give a ticket to heaven for your determination and tolerance?

v. If the world was ending tomorrow, would you rehearse playing dead on the couch, only to drift off to sleep a few moments later because you're aware how a power nap is important before death or would you get ready for the last day so as to not let your clumsy self show itself before the grim reaper?

vi. If the world was ending tomorrow, would you knock at the house of the one you love dearly and find her gone to the one she loves back, only to be realized not every love is ever reciprocated or would you fall in arms of the ones you call family aware that sometimes it's pleasant to expect love in return?

vii. If the world was ending tomorrow, would you, for once, enjoy a no regrets sunset and believe that you deserve all the kindness you give out to the world or would you dive in a sea of how-you-could-have-a-better-life knowing you're not to take that life to the path of mortality.

viii. If the world was ending tomorrow, wouldn't you be grateful for your existence, that no matter how hard things had been, how over the edge you were, you never gave up? Wouldn't you be proud of yourself for holding on after all? Wouldn't you be happy that you lived a life of happiness and pain, as a whole being? For in the end, that's what matters.

—**Saif Madre**

They're lying, aren't they?

The water was deep and flowing
When I accidentally pushed you in
And then the water was red
Because the stones cracked
Your skull open wide
I stood all this while silently
As tears uninvited greeted my cheeks.

Beautiful wildflowers grow untamed
And so were you one
But you were tortured and tamed
By people supposed to love you
To a extent that you were tired of existence
And so I wonder, was it an accident
Or you jumped to a tragic death

I was supposed to wear a suit
To your gloomy funeral
But I saw sanguine silhouettes
Of you pulling me towards that river bank
Where you took your last breath

And you seemed happy finally
Smiling in your blood stained dress

You never ceased to appear to me
Whispering as we strode down the lanes
You told me how beautiful afterlife is
And how burnt candles don't scare you now
You showed me your scars were healing
And how after a long time,
You looked forward to the dawn of the day

They told me you're unreal
And I am just imagining
Holding your hand
And walking on the banks of rivers
They say you're a fragment of illusion
On my mind platter
Because my mind is twisted in wrong ways

It's both a blessing and a curse
To feel everything so deeply
Because while I long to see you everyday
People tell me I'm going mad
And it's not love but grief
That you appear to me
They're lying, aren't they?

I confront you about the doubts

And you break down silently
And take me to the graveyard
I ask if it's a goodbye and you nod
I watch you floating down your tomb
And all this while I stand silently
As tears uninvited greet my cheeks.

—Saif Madre

love makes you do crazy things

i want to tell you
that i hate you
and your crooked smile
and gleaming eyes
how you don't look like
a glimpse of heaven to me
neither a hurricane of desire erupts
in the unholy confinement of my body
when i tousle your untidy hair
with angry streaks of red,
i want to tell you
how much of a god awful thing you're
but all i end up saying,
whispering in your ears is
a soft i love you.
it is common knowledge
that the space between two people
can be measured by the number of times

they look at each other and feel nothing
and i wish we were world's apart like that
for loving you is like
sitting patiently with knives in my chest
and every time you turn them
i despise you but myself more
for letting you do this.
love makes you do crazy things
and my mind is still stuck
in the bunk bed of the asylum we grew up in
you seem like the ring bearer
of the circus of my heart
my ghost filled eyes plead mercy
and a little bit of love
as a compensation to your cruelty
but love has never been
one of the many languages you speak
while desperation is the one i excel at.

—**Saif Madre**

If love was human

You know, I wonder sometimes if love was human, it would be one annoying person feeding hopes and lovely possibilities to our heart for days or months until it gets habitual only to then make our heart starve for eternity. Or maybe love as a person would have a keen interest in playing jenga with pieces of our heart, only to purposely pull the bottom most block with mischievous eyes and watching us building it all again with eyes wetted by glistening tears.

There is always closure hidden between notes in the song you randomly chose and words and verses that don't catch our attention the first time you come across it. So while I wiped the tears from the sleeve of my shirt, and packed the jenga of my heart giving up on the lost blocks, I write them all down in hope of finding myself in folded pages of old novels and long forgotten playlists on music apps that seldom might get open.

I open my diary, that was in the attic of a home we haven't set foot inside for years, to find it inscribed in scribbles and loops and some songs and words I wrote then for myself. I read it over and over again in solitude at the banks of river on a pleasant evening. I let my guard down and open my vulnerability at sunset for myself, risking the fact that emotions might have better of me. But some risks are worth taking, aren't they?

Is it supposedly normal to find another teenager your age on the exact place you regularly visit? I guess it's not because normal, out of all the adjectives in universe, doesn't go well with me. So I guess, destiny attempts to again feed my heart with a morsel it plans to take away later and hinting another chance at an already lost jenga game.

I remind myself to chew flecks of sugar on my tongue so that my vulnerability doesn't evolve into mere rudeness not excused by sweet sympathy. You know, precaution is better than cure right? I sit next to her and she smirks at me giving me a (maybe non existent) hint that she knows I sit here everyday. We make small talk sans awkwardness which being a first for me, makes me peculiar and she observes, but fails to mention or maybe choses not to.

It's been a year since I met her. I don't know her name yet but I know how long she cried when her dad left the family four years ago. She doesn't know my name either but is aware of the fact that nightmares greet me now and then and I have grown to their presence so much, that their absence makes me restless. We don't know each other's last name but we exchange diaries now and then to know which phrases made our heart stop and which particular words in a long lost song brings us peace. We don't know each other well but holding her hands brings me warmth on cold evenings.

—Saif Madre

A Forbidden Love Story
a short story

“Why did you call me here, Krish?” I ask him as he trudges inside the empty classroom, after it’s been nearly an hour since school ended.

“I want to talk to you. One last time.” He panted heavily, exhausted from playing football. His jersey sticked to his sweaty body, making his chest look a lot more brawny, making me resist my urges a lot more, so I don’t end up kissing him. I pry my eyes away from his body, that seemed to pull me in his embrace with my every look.

“I told you, there’s nothing to talk about. We should end what we have right now, right here.”

“I am here for closure, Aman.” He said sighing, and it pained me how calm and composed he sounded and how my squeaky voice was a sign of my cowardice.

“I don’t want any, nor should you.” I declare and walk to the door to leave.

"If you didn't, you wouldn't be here, knowing if someone saw us together again, they would send you away to the village." He countered and I realize how much I hate when he's right.

"We are both boys, Krish. A love like ours is forbidden. We are sinning. They're right to punish us." I give up and fall in his arms. My thin arms hold him close for one last time before they take him away from me. My eyes bleed a love I thought I would never experience.

"They do not define what's a sin and what's not. If us was a mistake, God would never have made us meet, would he?"

"I don't know. Abba doesn't talk to me anymore since the rumors spread and I can sense a look of disgust in Ammi's eyes when she serves me dinner. They wish I wouldn't have been born. I am a disgrace to them, Krish."

"If I wasn't an orphan, I would have convinced my parents to take you in but I promise I would do something to save you. To save us. We don't have to suffer an eternity of agony for just loving each other, Aman."

"There's no way out of this. We are doomed. Ammi's elder sister brought someone to pull the negative aura out of me, that's making me like this. How do I tell every part of me is filled with their so called negative aura and to pull it out means to destroy my soul in a thousand pieces."

"I wish people wouldn't take it as a duty to categorize love in boxes that fall as right or wrong in their perspectives." He grunted in anger.

"I wish a love like ours was normal." I whispered.

"Maybe it's not meant to be. A love like ours might be forbidden to the universe, but to us, it's extraordinary." He said and his words bring me warmth no fire is capable of.

We stay in each other's arms unknown if it's the last time we meet. I tucked the closure Krish wished to have, in the pockets of his shirt, a letter that he would read if we are broken apart by stereotypes again, and for the last time. And when I finally found peace, hell unleased it's wrath upon us as the door to the classroom was banged by fists that sounded familiar to me.

Abba broke open the door with two men and we were beaten to a pulp. The two men took me home and were told that Abba would deal with Krish. I didn't realize when I fell unconscious crying out for him. I woke up to my mother cleaning my wounds.

"Is he dead?" I ask her.

"No. Your father wouldn't kill anyone. It's a sin."

"So killing is a sin, but harming someone to a extent that they wish death upon themselves is not." I ask her, angry and she stays quiet.

"You hate me too right?" I ask her again.

"I would never. I just want you to know the path you chose is not right. I am just trying to guide you."

"I would consider your words if you answer my questions." I tell her and she nods.

"My love for a another boy is wrong, but Abba hitting you everyday is right?"

She looks at me, in horror as her belief that I'm oblivious to his torture was broken.

"I made a mistake. I deserved it."

"What about didi? He hits her with a belt when she returns late even though she just was with her friend, studying for exams."

"I have to make dinner, I should leave." She says and gets up to leave.

"Just because he prays doesn't mean he is innocent. God would never forgive him. And ignoring his sins and calling me out on mine is a sin too, Ammi. A bigger one than mine." I say out loud as she leaves, but I know for a fact, that she heard me.

We sit at the dinner table and all we hear is clanking of forks and spoons. Abba breaks the ice by declaring his plans for me.

"I am sending you to village to live with my elder brother. He will bring you in shape and educate him. He will take away all your bad thoughts and cleanse you from your sins."

"You should pay a visit to him too then." I whisper as he drinks his glass of water.

He looks at me with disgust and leaves the table mid dinner. I assume he went for washroom but he doesn't return.

"You should leave now." Ammi says.

"Where?"

"Away from here. I mixed a high dosage of sleeping pills in his water. He would not wake up soon."

"It could harm him."

"It would be the punishment for his sins. Punishment for hurting all of us. It was something I should've done a long time ago. Keep this money and leave this town as soon as you can."

"But he will hurt you and didi. I don't want you both to suffer for me." My eyes glisten with tears. Tears of love and fear.

"He wouldn't. I am getting him behind bars. Your sister got a job a week ago and she will be earning more than your Abba ever did. We will keep visiting you."

"Thank you Ammi."

"I can't promise you a happy ending with him but I assure you will live a life better than you did all these years."

—**Saif Madre**

When you fall in love with a writer

i. Writers all over the world aren't the same. Some write pickup lines in their diaries hoping they'd use it someday while some confess their love over open mics. Some are passionate lovers, showing you every sunset to exist while some steal quick kisses under the yellow halogen lights when you look into their eyes. But nevertheless they all would snatch their heart out and place it in your hands, just to feel the warmth of your hands on their cold blood pumping organ.

ii. A writer might not seem romantic at the first sight. They might be reluctant to talk or speak up, afraid they'd seem boring or maybe they would be too much fun to be with, that you couldn't imagine them writing a ode to one's they love. But with writers, you never know. Because they would be writing a fictional love letter just after a bad breakup or maybe they'd write a sonnet to a lost love while they hold hands with you.

iii. When you fall in love with a writer, be ready for enduring hard days with nagging insecurities. Because with them, it wouldn't always be little notes with messages of love and cotton candy kisses, but sometimes you feeling alone while they have a date with their quill. For when you hold their hands, get ready to whisper if you REALLY like their haiku on afterlife or reading the novellas they bought for you when they can't sleep.

iv. When a writer falls in love with you, it won't take you long to get used to letters of their obsession over you and they would know you'd smile wide everytime. They'd love you and yet let you have their space because they would know how love isn't the centre of universe, that the friendship between joey and chandler isn't any less important than the love between romeo and juliet, that there is a fine line between second chances and toxicity. Because when a writer loves you, you would encounter tweaking reality and hopeless romance at the same time.

v. When a writer mentions about you in their writings, you would know it's the right time. The right time to take out the love in a torn photograph you'd kept away until you find the courage to let someone touch your core with their bare fingers, to be vulnerable and intimate with deepest secrets that your soul still holds you guilty for.

vi. Because when a writer takes you in their arms, they wouldn't make promises of an eternity. They'd tell you how forever is a big concept, painted by alluring thoughts of everyday morning breakfasts and hiding the metaphors of broken cups and saucers. They'd tell you how they would love you day by day until they run out of words permanently to write about you and how seldom a writer falls short of words.

—**Saif Madre**

Is this what they call deja vu?

I lay in my bed staring nowhere
There is tension in the air
And a sense of familiarity
For I have experienced this before
Somewhere in my agonizing passive past
What was happening to me?
Is this what they call dèja vu?

I stand before the grave
Of my mother whom I never met
And memories flush me
From the cloud of gloom
Of a funeral I never went to
What was happening to me?
Is this what they call dèja vu?

The cafe reeks of loneliness
When I step in by the door
My chaotic mind greets me by illusions
Of a love who was never mine

A love radiant of honeysuckle happiness
What was happening to me?
Is this what they call dèja vu?

Doodles that are all over my skin
Inscribes names I never read
But remember as if they belong to me
I grin, reliving those times
That I have never once been in
What was happening to me?
Is this what they call dèja vu?

I am once again traumatized
By inhuman shadows embracing me
As if I am one of their own
And I try to resist
But my hold on sanity slips away again
What was happening to me?
Is this what they call dèja vu?

My body puts up a fight against me
And my conscience resists
I am afraid of the war
For I know the end is of me
But suddenly I feel freedom
Maybe I knew what was happening to me
Maybe this is what they call a dream

I wake up, sweating all over
Glad that the nightmare ceased
Before my sanity did
But there is still tension in the air
And yet a sense of familiarity
What was happening to me?
Is this what they call dèja vu?

—**Saif Madre**

Let's write an ode

Let's write an ode to all the things beautiful
And the melodious pain strumming in our ears
To rage trembling behind every chaos
To the black and white,
And the grey in all of us
Let's write an ode
To the ying and yang that is our life

Let's write an ode to the chambers of our heart
Where love persists to exist
To lovers and the ones being loved
To the moon, to whom ocean pleaded stay
To a home far away from home, in them
Let's write an ode
To the mere oxytocin we call love

Let's write an ode to the chains around our demons
To the eyes that ache with the weight of unshed tears
To the purple bruises on our vulnerability
To smiling face that don't trust anymore

To those jealous of death
Let's write an ode
To the ones who survived, nevertheless

Let's write an ode to mortal writers
Taking a step towards immortality with phrases
To the thought of losing our muse
Everytime a block latches on our mind
To unwritten words and disguises of fiction
Let's write an ode
To the pen that bleeds our darkest insecurities

Let's write an ode to what could have been
To the possibilities and such
Of our choices and paths
To the echoes that fade away
Of hope and recklessness
Let's write an ode
To regrets that serve as our middle name

Let's write an ode to the nostalgia that breeds
From under the closet in the attic
To the old perfume bottles nd albums long forgotten
To all our visceral hope's and dreams
Destined to fulfill someday day or other
Let's write an ode
To the simpler times of our lives

Let's write an ode to the universe
Of which we are a part of
To the light that scatters, just like us
To the sun under our umbrella's
And the sky so vast, holding us within
Let's write an ode
To our prolonged existence, until the moon stops shining.

—**Saif Madre**

and as you grow up, you grow apart

what was life when you were an ickle little bean? when happiness was in existence and sadness an occasional passer by. when crying was no sin and anger, an emotion justified. don't we all have certain flashbacks of the time when dependency was not a burden and maturity a concept for the far future? but with every moment that passed, you walked towards a supposedly mature life. you believed it would be a bliss, growing up. but disappointments are inevitable, aren't they?

while you believed an illusion termed as "forever", the books kept on getting thicker. but as puberty hit and your face were fashioned with zits, your heart broke when whom you called a best friend, did not consider to call you for a party. the thesaurus called it a misunderstanding but you were convinced it was a betrayal. you never talked and they found it more comforting to forget you while glimpses of your friendship haunted you on school nights. introversion became not a choice but an obligation when you had no one to share your sandwiches with. and you never realized when you started missing your childhood.

loneliness found a abode within you, and your feelings of distraught fell hurriedly on the pages of your diary. you wrote everyday, but you ripped off more pages than you wrote. what if someone rea? if they got an insight of what goes inside in your mind? it would be terrible, to have someone look around the chamber of your memories, the intrusion guilty of hanging the accused to death. your family asked you, if you were okay, when you didn't eat your favourite, and you murmured an "i am okay" vaguely but sometime then those words stamped on your tongue and you haven't stopped since.

the unfamiliarity from your peers didn't stop you from tripping into love. it was found to be literal, when a certain ditch on an annoying rainy day, caught your shoes, causing you to fall over the mud. but the irritation wiped off your face, when your eyes fell on the person in front of you. they handed you their handkerchief, out of casual humanity but your hopeless heart took it as a hint. after cleaning up, you returned to hand them back their belonging, but it broke your pitiful heart when you found they were spoken for by someone who was not you. being the rebel you're, you never returned their handkerchief. it still resides in your top drawer.

do you remember when you lashed out on someone and there were a lot of surprised faces? was it because you had always told yourself to keep your emotions in check and to retain a pretentious smile no matter what. the aforementioned actions makes the witnesses believe you're content with life and would take no interest in intruding within. people like chaos, it makes the mundancy of their life a little interesting, and gives them the mandatory satisfaction that their life is better. but when you let the wildness unleashed, there are a lot of prying eyes. apologies work well in keeping the normal intact but you could always stare like an axe murderer and none would dare would question you. appealing enough?

but you stop growing up after a span of time, your limbs are as stretched as they could be, your mind assumed to carry the weight of your parent's unfulfilled dreams. but your heart is still fragile, hanging on a thread. you try no more to find a shelter for it, for you believe that you would never belong. it is a thought screwed to deepest of your soul and no reassurance has never been capable of causing a dent. you believe you're a lost cause, and your therapist agrees while they would never accept. but being a human, you hold the human tendency to blame. you blame yourself, your peers, diaries, parents, teachers, your dentist you haven't seen for 2 years. but most of all, you blame time. perhaps if you were still a child, it would be okay. but time passed, and as you grew up, you grew apart.

—Saif Madre

the ways i'd love you

i. i'd look in your eyes and never look away

beauty attracts eyes and mine have found it's abode in your hazel irises. there is a certain silence when we just sit there, look at each other as your lips brush against mine and my heart flutters and leaves sparks off the rigged edges. there had be chaos wrecking the world apart, but i'd find my peace in you. i'd close my eyes and still see you, because you never leave the back of my head, because you're the light in all of my darkness, because you're the dream for me that came true.

ii. i'd recite poetries i write for you

aren't they beautiful? the verses they write for you and me, our love. so i would write for you too, for the way your face reddens up when your name aligns mine, pleases my heart to a hundred degrees. i'd write an ode for the biscuit crumbles falling off your lips, i'd weave a sonnet for the times you dance randomly, i'd dedicate a prose for your morning face with the wild strands of your hair on your face. i'd write a story of how i am the bohemian outcast, and you the generous neighbour who took me in. and i'd write a haiku for the home i find in your arms.

iii. i'd sit under the stars with you

someday when our words would seem to be expired, i'd take your hand and pull you to the slippery terrace. you'd slip and despite my attempts, fall a painful tumble. i'd look at you apologetically and you with a grimace, would pull me down. everything would be alright as we had look at the stars, with a peace humanity never granted. i'd shout out to the sky that "i have a love in my life and it makes me stronger than anything you can imagine" you'd ask me who i was talking to, and i'd say the stars are jealous of me for their moon is away from them and mine is next to me.

iv. i'd let you take me to museums and temples

i have never been aware of the rules of religion but you'd take me to the temples and i'd nod for it would make you happy. we would sit there praying to the deity and somewhere sometime i'd thank him for bringing you in my fate. we would close our eyes and whisper our prayers in the almighty's ears, and the syllables of my name from your mouth and yours from mine and we'd smile inspite of ourselves. and looking at you, i'd chant your name like you're the only religion i know of.

v. i'd be the reason your insecurities don't exist anymore

of all the days you ask me why do you love me, i have recited answers from my heart. for the flaws that you tell me about yourself, all the wrong things you've done inspite of yourself, all the small mistakes for which you die a little everyday, it doesn't change the way i think about you. it would never add a tint to the beauty you're in my eyes. when i tell you, i love you, i mean that i love the good and bad, the ugly and sad, leaving not a part of you out. so when you tell me of your scars, i'd tell you how they remind me of the crescent moon, when you tell me that you have toxicity in your veins, i'll tell you how i would kiss you pure.

vi. i'd show little gestures to potray my love

aren't there times when we walk together? your hands clasped in mine and our words weaved through a loom of silence, while the only sound piercing the silence would be the leaves crumbling beneath our feet. i'd then whisper to you, how it feels as if we know each other from our past lives, for the familiarity i seek in you never even lies within myself. someday i'd ask you to guess my favourite colour and the first name you take would be by beloved then. someday i'd ask you of your favourite book, and recite you lines from them next day. someday i'd make you a list of promises with only intent of fulfilling them, while the last one would ask not a forever, but that i'd give you the same love till all is left in me, is your name on my tongue and hollow eyes looking for you.

—Saif Madre

Cereal Killer short story

And I ran my hands over my hair as I completed replying to my fan mails. It was unexpected that I would be replying to a fan mail addressed to ME?! I just wrote a thriller novel and published it. And it just by chance hitted the bestsellers list and my face was all over the newspapers. Nothing much. To be honest, the casualty of writing this doesn't do justice to my residing excitement.

So a couple of months earlier, I started investing my time in writing to get over the saudade of losing my mother recently. Though it seemed impossible once, I wrote my first book and my dad made me publish it because after a long time of my disinterest in anything, I had shown interest in something and being the proud father he was, he wanted to publish it. And me being the under confident geek, didn't expected it to get popular. But when it did my happiness knew no bounds.

The book was titled "Cereal Killer." Yeah, not serial, but cereal killer. It was a strange story which makes me more confused that how did it progress so much. The story was about a strange ghost like person made of cereal who goes on killing people randomly. Also he was made of cereals and his veins flowed with cereals rather than blood. He would vomit cereals on the victims until it blocked their ways of breathing hence choking them to death. Such an unusual(and gross) way of murder right?

I was enjoying the glory until one morning, a death had been reported in the newspaper. A person choked to death and his food pipe was found blocked by cereals. I thought it was just a coincidence and the person must have eaten too much of cereals at the same time. But my self assurance was shook by another same news on the television.

The deaths had taken the name of murders now. And I was afraid, I could be blamed for suggesting a way for murders. My days were filled with guilt. But one day, the television bore the news that it was the same person killing all the people and there was an attempt to shoot him but the bullet when through him and a couple of cereals fell on the ground. And that meant, he was immortal. And the very moment, I regretted the ending I wrote. The ending which showed how he wouldn't be defeated and leave the town leaving hundreds dead.

Terrified I went to bed thinking of writing a sequel to end the Cereal Killer's life but as I started dusting my bed. Loads of cereal fell down from the blanket. Terrorized by this, I started going to call my dad when the glass of water fell on floor. I started cleaning the glass and the glass cut my skin and I expected blood to flow out. But all that came out was cereals. And I realized. I was the Cereal Killer after all.

—Saif Madre

unshared excerpts that I never meant to write

i. of the forlorn loneliness i drown in

i wonder what we all are but lonely miscreants suffering in guilt at the hour of twilight. we are millions of people yearning, looking to others to satisfy us, yet isolating ourselves with misery when someone holds up a hand to us. my clock ticks with a sound audible like never before, as it sears through the silence i found myself comfortable in. if i were a planet, i'd be mercury, far from moons to revolve around me. i wish for someone to stand by me, but if they do, the air i share with them suffocates me.

fiction denies to wrap me up in its blankets, telling me it's for my own good. but only if it knew I prosper from destruction of my own.

ii. of the misery i inherited

disappointment. that's what i have grown to be. my muses have grown stale in the pool of my own blood. they stink of lies and manipulation that i admit to whisper in my own ears. what other way is there to dodge the bruises on my slacked body. my mother hates my teeth, afraid i presume, that they would grow as twisted as me, resistant to give in to her pleas stinking of harrowing sympathy for herself. my father's stubbornness flows through my putrid veins, so does his hesitation to act upon it. we both long for something that was ripped from our fates, peace. but stubborn as we are, we still look for it.

iii. of nightmares and haunting aftermaths

what would you choose? terror or the restlessness from it? for i have grown to the nightmares, i have acquainted with the demons that chase me through the night and the cracks of the desolated grave with my name on it are familiar to me. but what makes me afraid are the days that are darker than the night. normalcy is abnormal to me, and the alive deadlier than those who departed. sweat runs through my forehead in dreams with lavender fields and sugar and brownies, for i am afraid of the poison glazing in them. i fear only the horrors that sprout from goodness and hope.

iv. of prolonged existence and delayed mortality

what do we really fear death? or the consequences of it? the pain searing through our body as we feel the life seeping through us. we fear to leave behind memoirs of us, people who would be haunted by our absence, or worse the realization that it would budge none. we live on and on, day by day, making dreams of the far fetched future when the next second holds the capability of ending us. parts of us wants to know how to bring back the dead, because to dream of impossible is our tendency. but what is life if not anticipation of death.

v. of selfish desires and selflessness on a high horse

i loathe it how emotions are pushed into boxes of positive and negative, and the mere hunch of the claimant cynical ones label us as bad people. how is rage termed as bad, when the act of suppressing it destroys us from within? how is jealousy supposed to destory a person when no signs of it is as synonymous to indifference? how is hope so beautiful, decorated with all pretty adjectives when it creates a void in us longing to be fulfilled? why is being selfish defined as downfall of others but all the emptiness selflessness is capable of neglected as under the cover of heroism? why are emotions restraint to personalities, and the lack of supposedly positive ones makes us look unhinged.

vi. of incomplete words that complete me

aside from skeletons in my closet, my home also provides a shade to my torn manuscripts, and the quills that pull a caution tape around my heart. but being a writer is tiring, when all the self doubt washes upon my want to write more. if i could draw a self portrait of an author that is to be me, i would scribble my insecurities, for they're what that waters the blooming metaphors i write. i am sorry but not sorry for the illicit affair i harbour with dark corners of my sanity, writing death and taking joy in it. i am far from ashamed of my bleeding vulnerability that's coming undone as i write of the knots in my stomach, untying it strand by strand. and maybe i wouldn't know ever of how to live sans words, for what would i breathe if not the metaphors clutching for my dear life.

—Saif Madre

The girl who loved the demon

When you'll tell me you love me
I'll place my fingers on your lips
And ask you not to repeat again
Because by loving me
You'd fall on a path of despair
And you should swallow back the words
Or the poison you'd spit would taint your own destiny.

You're a person destined with happiness
Watering dancing daffodils in gardens
So don't throw all that away
By falling in love with me
For I wake among dead weeds
And that I could destroy you
Petal by petal, fern by fern.

Walk off the threshold
Of the home I built of stones
Stones that cement my heart
Before I make you broken promises

Like I made to the ones before you
For I know the end of us
And it's certainly not pleasant

When you paint me in rainbow hues
I would run away from you
And dive in a jar of molten lava
So that the fire would melt the love
You carved with your paintbrushes
And all that would be left
Would be the burning scars on my body

When you find me catching fireflies
And writing sonnets on love
Don't mistake me for someone soft
With a broken heart
Because you haven't seen me yet
Burning the sonnets I write
And killing the fireflies I found

Can I ask you?
How are you capable
Of making love out of hate?
Because all I have ever given you
Are cold stares and dagger stabs
Yet you don't cease to stick around
Are you the definition of insanity?

When they write about us
In the history books
I hope they would mention
How I warned you that I'm hostile
But it was you who took your risks
Of loving a demon only to be called
The girl who loved the demon.

—Saif Madre

my lover

my lover is a metaphor
i have written in a hurry
frivolous as a hopeless dreamer
a perspective too blurry.
my lover is the warmth of April
and the drizzle of July
my favourite grey among black and whites
a souvenir to remember by.
my lover is a reckless rebel
pursued when i dared to be bold
made of rules meant to be broken
but secretly lending hands to hold.
my lover blesses the dark
afraid of the light
a spawn of the devil
an inhabitant of the night.
my lover has the sweet tooth
for love and its grand gestures
pretending to show a solemn face

but going scarlet when our souls conjure.
my lover is neon lights
in a dark space
less of hope, more of chaos
with a 'would make you smile' face.
my lover is the sorrow swallowed
by the weeping night sky
tasting of guilty pleasures
and reeking of hardest goodbyes.
my lover is the stars in my sky
tugging love notes in my pockets
dedicating playlists and incomplete poetries
and gifting heart-shaped lockets.
my lover is God's best creation
a raw piece of art
my lover seems to find their home
in the soft corners of my heart.

—**Saif Madre**

my lover part 2

my lover is all things beautiful
with a hint of honest modesty
the universe in the palm of their hand
a soul brimming of curiosity.
my lover is the morning dew
adorning the trees at the break of dawn
up at the strangest hours
smelling of blue skies yawn.
my lover has a fork for a tongue
with their star speckled eyes
sarcasm, a sacred language
with sudden exasperated sighs.
my lover is wrapped in summer clouds
a sunflower tucked in their hair
they are the sweet blueberry dreams
in the field of worst nightmares.
my lover is the haze behind my ribcage
a voracious desire of my beating heart
my lover tugs at the black strings of fate

every moment we stay apart.
my lover is the reason
my cheeks are red when i smile
the cause of my impatience
when i don't see them for a while.
my lover takes my name in a melody
of our most beloved song
their eyes are my salvation
their arms are where i belong.
my lover hides anguish under their fingerprints
despite an everlasting smile on their face
never failing to bring one mine
in a hundred different ways.
my lover looks at me
with a sense of adoration
whispering silent promises
how i will always be "the one".

—Saif Madre

my lover part 3

my lover looks at me
when I'm drifted and unaware
planting soft kisses on my palms
invoking our illicit affairs.
my lover tastes like cigarettes
on a stormy midnight
revisiting old memories
of falling in love at first sight.
my lover tells me
my dreams taste like ash
burning by the flame of love
only to be put out in a flash.
my lover is my wish on an eyelash
i made when i was nine
breaking a hundred other hearts
only to save the glory of mine.
my lover dances like crazy
when it's just my eyes watching
as smooth with my forgotten guitar

plucking my heartstrings.
my lover is a midas desperation
i can never not touch
sheltered in their welcoming arms
a vow to never budge.
my lover is the answer
to the questions in my eyes
says honesty cuts like a rusted knife
but is made up of the prettiest lies.
my lover is my first dance
and the last one i want to be kissing
as cheesy as it may sound
it's someone I would never stop missing.
my lover's name is the title
to my best poem ever
says promises are miserable
but always whispers sweet forevers.

—**Saif Madre**

kiss me

kiss me to the verge of silence
as if your lips would be guilty of violence.
kiss me till my words melt in your mouth
silent promises with no trace of doubt.
kiss me as i make you my religion
a fluttering sunflower to warmth of your sun.
kiss me a shrine to flourish my sins
the reason behind my red cheeks and lopsided grins.
kiss me when the flowers of spring bloom
a gleam of hope in a nightmare of gloom.
kiss me where the grass is greener and sky cloudy blue
even in places where affection is considered taboo.
kiss me and intertwine our scarred hands
in the heat and breeze of golden sands.
kiss me till i cry out my heart
a lingering souvenir on days we are apart.
kiss me sweeter than the taste of wine
till every poem start to taste like your name with mine.

—**Saif Madre**

"Can we hold hands?"

"Can we hold hands?" You asked me and I nodded

My hands were trembling with relentless anxiousness but the touch of your hand on mine sent shivers down me, calming me down. We were sitting by a cliff, with our belongings aside us, including one monumental cactus, a gift from you. You told me, "when all roses withers, this would persist. And how they both gave thorns, at least a cactus wouldn't hide it's. I catch you smiling at me but you don't look away, you don't hide your love in crypts and secrets. You wink at me and I think how fates may not be as cruel as we believe.

When we sit in our comfortable silence, you glance at me with a cunning smirk. Not so later, you hand me a ransom note and ask me to sign it. I read how you have written to my mother, telling her that you also ask for your rights on me, that I am now to be shared, if not taken away by you forever. I roll my eyes at you while thinking how gratitude is one word, insufficient to hold my bursting emotions for you. You rip the letter after a while, saying perhaps you'd say this to my mother, not in ink but in person.

Promises and misery lie interwoven to each other. Except a promise can be broken but misery? It is eternal. So when you tell me, "I can promise you" I ask you not to. For promises loosen the thread of love and recklessness, hope pulling at both ends. I tell you how the memories of past lovers have been burnt away from my chest but all they leave is scars of unmade promises. You understand and not complain, looking me in eyes, pulling me closer and whispering to me,

"I promise, I wouldn't make any promises."

Of all the days you sleep with your head on my shoulder, I am afraid I cannot get any work done. I mean, how could anyone? Your eyelashes strum against your closed eyes and I collect the broken ones so we have a wish to spare. There is something very gentle in your rhythmic breaths involving a snort here and there. I tease you of it later and you swear you do not snore but the teasing persists. Some days when fortune is abundant on me, you talk in your sleep and I would be lying if I do not hear syllables of my name from your mouth. Looking at you, I realize how love falls heavier on a weighing scale if I have you beside me.

Poets often say, that love reeks of pain. Or perhaps it is the other way round. Would it be life if there are no hardships on every nook of it? I have pockets full of love for you and my wardrobe is scratched with your initial on places my mother wouldn't care to check, but still it is human tendency to adorn rage under our fingertips and an uncompromising temper under our clean breaths. There are moments when we fight, argue and not talk to each other. We go our ways, rant of each others shortcomings for flaws are not always the most beautiful, and end up crying but not talking. But may it be a sideway glance or perhaps a snapshot by the sunset, smiles are exchanged and love flourishes after all as I come back to a home that is you.

—Saif Madre

some kill sans daggers.

the hospital lights reflected grey. the miserable kind of grey that seemed to poke at your agonies till it got the better of you. one would say it was strange how I was not so long back dancing and now i, picked on my nails till the throbbing cuticles abandoned the storm that punctured the air out of my stomach. it started out as a good day, best one rather. but too much happiness is sometimes unstable, it topples over to something worse.

i remember how my dad cupped my face as he told me i would be getting a sister in less than a day. like every typical toddler, i asked him where did she come from and my dad laughed it off. we drived up to the hospital, holding hands and while my mother cried in pain, we could feel the aura of happiness simmering around her. they wheeled her into the big rooms as we sat out. i counted the tiles to make enough of this unending time and sometime then i was afraid. what if they wouldn't love me enough? what if i was replaced? did the naive me ever realize how she wished the baby never came?

you know, sometimes fate plays jokes on us? jokes that rip apart our lives with no regret whatsoever? so it did with me, as the one wish i made in absolute misery was chosen as an initiative to prove god really exists. it didn't take much than a sullen faced doctor to tell us the worst of what we could hear. widest of smiles fell to deepest of frown and i kept tapping on to my chest, asking the despair and guilt to leave me alone, for it does take not old enough for someone to know that some kill sans daggers.

as we drove home then, the silence stretched into my eardrums. i tried to outstretched my arms but there was no space with the knocking despair in the crevices of my chest. i hugged my mother, but she felt too stiff to reciprocate my affection. it seemed as if with the death of my little sister who never saw the world, so arrived the passing of her empathy and love. i had never seen my father crying but when he never left the bathroom till later and once his well kept hair now fell over his face like wild strands, i hated the fates for fulfilling a wish I'd never really made.

as days followed, so did pity calls. my aunt cried out her heart to my mother as she sat cold, out of any tears to shed. my father came late from work, for there was no way but to drown into burden of his workload so none asked how he really was. my teacher never asked me for days and weeks, why my plaid skirt was not clean enough and my pigtails improper by the school standards. my grandmother too offered her condolences, but it was common knowledge that she was the only one who took some joy with the knowledge there was not another granddaughter for her to marry off.

with days, years passed in no time. there were still fresh scars on my chest, scars of the time i pricked on my heart to let out the guilt and regrets. the regret that it was my mistake i could never tell my secrets to another soul, that i couldn't tell her about menses and self respect, that love is wild and dangerous. i wished i had the courage to tell my mother and father it was all my fault, but they were too distant now, despite being in the next room. the indifference of them ate me alive and the punishment of my sin while felt right, was too cold for my fragile heart.

someday when i was as old as my mother, it was believed i was pregnant again. my first daughter held the name of the sister i never had. it was again a happy day, but i tried to silence them for i was afraid too much of joy can jinx us again. we again drove to the hospital, and history repeated in front of my eyes. but it was now my responsibility to let my elder daughter know how worthy she is. it was none but my burden to not let her make the mistake that ruined all of me.

—Saif Madre

When we lay down under the sky

When we lay down under the sky
Ask me a hundred questions
And I would treat you
To a picnic to past serendipities
On the day when I wrote first
And I might push you off the cliff
Of the memories that screamed misery

When we lay down under the sky
Hold my hand tightly
And watch me flinch slowly
Because it might burn my insides
Suddenly getting all too vulnerable
But don't worry, I would loosen up
And maybe clasp your fingers too

When we lay down under the sky
I might confide in you

How I am a stack of dominoes
Where blankets of sarcasm
Lay above my irrelevant insecurities
And how I wait, someone would pull
The right piece for an impending eternity

When we lay under the sky
Recite me a poem I wrote
About hugging the horizons
Because I never remember
What I carve on the white paper
And your voice brings me peace
Peace I longed to embrace

When we lay under the sky
Sing me a song
Maybe "A thousand years"
Meaning every verse of it
And promise me that it will never end
Because I might suffer from a nasty habit
Of believing in forevers meant to end

When we lay under the sky
Please neglect the absence of colour
On my translucent body

Because I'm just a muse painted
On the black canvas of the universe
And I am afraid I'll cease to exist
The day the sky falls upon us.

—Saif Madre

The universe within me

I am made of all things unusual
A human by birth
But an art crafted through years
The meteors crash on my skin
Making way to a soul
Too naive for earthly miseries
But bright enough nevertheless

Little stars adorn my forehead
Fallen from an infinity
Forgotten by the sky so vast
I tell them how it's okay
That the forgotten is always the most precious
And they whisper to my mortal ears
That it's enough I remember them alone.

I stare at the pearl moon
And it returns my gaze sharply
Rising high tides of the metallic emotions within
I hold my stomach as it churns

And find craters within it
I find it quite suprising
How they're empty yet so full

Lullabies of the moon bless my ears
As my subconsciousness delves into the night
I hold back myself before I get lost
Among the folds of constellations
That the sky beholds beautifully
My heart feels a twinge of pain
Only if I was brave enough to lose myself in it

The sun is too bright
For my sins to be absolved
My spirit attempts to escape
Sick of the sun and planets
But I walk upon them barefoot
And the burning rage takes it all away
The regret and guilts, off my chest

There is a home waiting for me
Up above the clouds
Where peace would find me
Sans any hope, sans any expectations
A home where solitude isn't punished
And miseries aren't flaws anymore
But I wonder why do they call it hell

The self hatred residing in me
Dissolves into nothingness
As nature embraces, stars my crown
I am closer to the moon and sky
Than the earth could ever dare to be
I feel invincible for now
I behold the universe within me.

—**Saif Madre**

"are we too young for this?"

"are we too young for this?" you asked me as we walked by the aisle surrounded by empty chairs. a day more and it would be our wedding. one we had been awaiting for so long. but your question unnerved me, brought up questions i never thought.

"why do you a-ask?" i managed to stammer.

"marriage is too big of a commitment, are we ready?" you said.

"are we?" i asked, with goosebumps dominant which people otherwise called wedding jitters.

it wasn't that i never had second thoughts, but looking at a girl i have loved since she broke a bully's nose just because he stole my lunch made it all go away always. but now i did think, i thought of every thing that would be different. that i would have to be a changed man, and handle responsibilities, that mistakes i make could only have so much consequences that i could deal with. that....

"are you okay?" you held my hand and i felt peace blooming over me.

"yes, it's just, everything will be different now."

"change is inevitable. there are good parts too, like we can live together. no more sneaking around." you said as you held my hand more tightly, interlacing our fingers.

"what if our careers steer us in opposite directions?"

"I'll watch you sleep on a skype call."

"i- how do you have answers for everything?" i grinned despite myself. suddenly i knew why i wasn't worried all along. the universe could be brimming with questions but i would somehow find the answers in your eyes.

"let's move to the top of a mountain." you whispered as we lay down on the ground outside, stargazing at the constellations of innocence, whose names we were oblivious of.

"you know right that there would be no bakeries nearby to satisfy your midday cravings?"

"ahh, that's a real bummer."

"have you written your vows?" i asked, out of sheer curiosity.

"i copied them off internet." she giggled as i stared surprised.

"wait, you too?" i joked as we burst out of laughing.

once the laughter calmed, i fished out crumpled pages out of my back pocket and handed them to her.

"aren't you supposed to read them to me tomorrow?" you asked.

"does your curiosity permit that?"

"i think not." you said and read the paper out loud.

"i will always love you a little more than i did the day before."

"i could write you a perfectly made list of vows just like they show you in movies and books. but i am a person and sometimes a terrible one at that. sometimes recklessness could get better of me and risk breaking all of the promises I've made, which i do not wish to do. but even if the hell breaks loose, the one thing i know is i would never stop loving you."

—Saif Madre

i see you waiting for someone

i see you waiting for someone
four tables apart
we are back to known strangers
of hazy memories and paining hearts.
we both felt abandoned
you by me, and me by love
i always wondered if our fates were wrecked
or did i not love you enough?
your brown eyes still stir me up
his name on your lips setting off a fire
how i wish it could be me
but it's hilarious isn't it? unwanted desire?
i never knew you noticed
the look in my eyes when i saw you
mistaken thoughts that i fell for you all over again
but i never stopped to start anew.
i wish you knew how i would lay
withered roses in your wake
travelling miles to make you happy

breaking my heart for your sake.
love is a concept foreign
but it spells by your name to me
stuttering confessions and bitten nails
a coward's attempt at bravery.
in a perfect alternate universe
you'd be holding my hands instead of him
sharing prolonged glances of love
one where it was me you told all your secrets and whims.

—**Saif Madre**

My therapist's assignment

It's funny how some beginnings are grand and some as simple as your next door neighbour asking for a cup of sugar. So is ours of how we meet in the abandoned aisle of a library, our chest stacked with literature that scream the words that don't leave our lips otherwise. I try to avoid you but I cannot. Your eyes bleed sunflowers and honey drips from the edges of your lips as you read the ever living poems of dead poets. You watch me looking at you but embarrassment seems to be my best friend now and I don't mind when you sit next to me and we argue of the sadism that exists in forlorn souls. I look at my phone and it's 5:03 pm and it's too late but you ask me for my number. I debate with every voice in my head but end up giving it since my therapist asked me to let love in again, and I decide that's what you'll ever be, my therapist's assignment.

I think of writing about you in my journal but I remember how I promised myself not to be miserable. Slowly, we keep meeting more and I can't help but like it. I start writing poems of your every fallen curl and how you let me clean the fog out your round glasses. I wonder if it is an act of manipulation or you really care about me tripping when you tie the laces on my mud stained sneakers. I have started loving you but I don't trust you for it's rare to be a nice person and rarer for one to fall in my arms. I tell you everything from my trust issues to the insecurities I everyday wash my face with and you hold your peace as we watch the apocalypse drinking beers on your roof.

Trust is a complicated concept but not to you. you decide to trust me first so I can trust you so you tell me how your sister is gay and your father a homophobe. You tell me how your mother worships silence as if no greater god could exist. You let me touch the bruises on your heart for the last girl you loved attempted to take your heart when she realised she had none of her own. You tell me everything and I don't remember when but i slice my chest apart for you to see. You stare in my eyes and pull out the fragments of grief sticking from my ribcage before melting the coldness settled inside of me. the next time I visit my therapist I tell her everything about you and how I dream of you even on nights I don't sleep and she praises me for the evolution in the assignment.

And one of the nights I am telling you of my favourite disaster when you call my name. it's in small whispers instead of screams and i flinch because warmth isn't what i have grown up with, but fire. when you ask me why, i tell you this is what my mother taught me and you tell me to unlearn it now that you're here. but tell me, how can someone unlearn the art of survival? I tell you how I am anxiety personified and you tell me you are good with handling the demons but I don't know how to tell you I don't have demons, it's me, I am the demon. So I don't say anything. You tell me you'll never leave and I almost laugh because love has never been this easy for me.

My brother tells me he likes you better than the last one and when I ask why, he says you are gentle, just the right amount for me. I smile thinking of you and play every word you say again and again in my mind. But somewhere I lose my nerve thinking I would lose you despite what you told me. as I said, I was never too big on trusting. I want to cry to the gods how the restlessness is a curse and they tell me I am no lesser of a sinner. When you visit me again i hug you before driving a rusted knife through your stomach. i pull you to the storage unit and build a shrine on your body. monday morning i visit my therapist and tell them the assignment failed again. she asks what happened and i tell her *how love is brutal, it kills everyone.*

—**Saif Madre**

an abandonment of your memories

and i sincerely hope
i don't remember you anymore
not the way you looked at me
with a honey coloured gaze
as if you'd surrender all your sanity
for the mere price of me
and certainly not the way you touched
the fragile bits with such tenderness
a salvation to my wounds
a meaning to my existence.
i bet we would be different people
if our paths had never crossed
and i wasn't a victim of the massacre
of your pink bicycle with a wicker basket
scraped knees and scattered apologies
the meeting of our eyes
and the longing that never went away
but if i wasn't yours, who would i be?

my bones have shattered
and muscles began to tire
still i cannot possibly clear off
the fine features of your face
from my cluttered mind
as if they have burned themselves
in the hollow confines of my chest
even the nails stuck on my ribcage
hang off bloody polaroids of us
the grief below my tongue
smells like your yellow sweater
and i still have rubberbands on my wrist
from the day you forgot to take it back.
i want to forget you and forget it all
but i was never the one to rip bandages
and forgetting you
would be like erasing myself
for all i am now is
an abandonment of your memories

—**Saif Madre**

on how to let go

i. cry till you run out of your tears

cry. cry and don't worry if it ruins your mascara or takes a dent at your mould of masculine ego. cry in a locked room with only a tub of chocolate ice cream despite your running nose and their half burnt pictures because you couldn't bring yourself to let your sole memories be a heap of ash. cry and bite your nails till they bleed and punch your scrawny arms into the concrete wall. cry again and again and again and again because that's the only thing you need to do sometimes, cry your heart out.

ii. step out of your safety island.

and finally when your repeated purchases of tissue boxes do not fall in line with your unconventional budget, put on a clean shirt that does not reek of their unkept promises and open your door. reply to those 173 messages your best friend left you to ask if you have killed yourself and tell them you need them to filth talk your way out of misery. reminiscence of a time wouldn't hurt before you started to believe the world was big and your existence too small to matter. but don't forget to buy another box of tissues on your way back because memories are sadistic and tears inevitable.

iii. dear diary, please listen to me

on days you come home to your empty bed that smells a lot like longing, pull out your chair and write yourself an obituary. write about their hazel eyes and the dead butterflies in your stomach. write about the mask you put on every morning because somehow two weeks is enough time to mourn the loss of a living person. write how you're so tired of being holy and hope suffocates you with it's pretty little fingers. write how you still murmur their name in your sleep so you stopped sleeping anymore. write of the grief latched in your throat as if you re wiping blood off your mouth for raw unspent love left to loiter always turns too tangible to avoid.

iv. have yourself a little campfire

on days you manage to close your eyes for a measly 10 seconds and manage to wake up without a tear stained pillow and a longing desperate to be fulfilled, celebrate whatever is left off your existence. go grocery shopping in your tracks and talk to your neighbours dog that could always appreciate another round of petting. drive to your father's old yard with every gift they gave you and burn all souvenirs they left you. paint yellow over the scars they left you and replace their angry words with sweet melodies from your spotify playlist. and just to be clear, abusing the existence of spotify ads is a healthy habit.

v. do not give up on love

sometime when all your feelings have been deflated and all their name brings about in you is a face of disgust and your memories starts to look a lot like regrets, know that you have escaped the burden of the sky full of misery they left for you. but days later when you stumble across someone else with similar brown hair and freckles that seem to shine when they smile, do not take a step back from letting love playing it's best tricks. bury the dead butterflies in corners you'll never look at again and let new ones be born in the confines of your ribcages. pull off the painted claws of hope from your neck and befriend it again for after a story ends, there always exists a epilogue you could write.

—**Saif Madre**

perhaps all i want to be is yours.

if i could turn all things i said drunk
in a poem
my fingertips would weave me a sonnet
that immortalise your hazel eyes
shining under the weight of falling stars
the ink of my quill would flow like blood
on a martyr's corpse
and sing a tale in your native tongue
of the unambiguous gestures of love
ever known to the entirety of humanity.
it is very often sometimes
that i don't find it very obvious what you want
for your lopsided smiles
entangle my longings in an immediate urge
to pull you in my arms and never let go
while the frowns that adorn your face
make me want to upturn the world
and tear the yarn of fates

perhaps all i want somedays is to be
the reason of your happiness
the shoulder for your agonies
perhaps all i want to be is yours.

—**Saif Madre**

you're a 10 but

you wake up every day holding hands of the ghost that haunted your nightmares and excuse their presence as if you deserve it, as if you deserve the punishment. you wash your face but leave your sins intact for you believe forgiveness is not yours to be asked for. your nails are bloody with all the scars you have tried to scrape off and knuckles a faded shade of crimson from all the confines you've attempted to escape.

your body is wrapped in cassette tapes of your favourite songs, those you could never sing aloud because your comfort was always strangled by the sense of insecurities. you colour your nails the colour of redemption but wear gloves to cover them. your eyes often are the door to your soul but you never forget to double lock the latch and tuck the keys in the deepest crease of your ribcage.

you dig up the grave of a mother who never knew you and narrate her the stories you write about serial killers for known strangers was the unfamiliarity you were always a little too familiar with. you sharpen your teeth with the indifference of your father and feed on the leftovers of the love you were starved of. you worship greek gods as you are intrigued by their flaws scrawled upon holy pages.

you never comb your hair, afraid that it will lose you a chance of them ruffling your hair playfully. you cry in your bathtubs of a love too unrequited to be ever considered real but who would understand the cracks on your vulnerability other than you. you swallow pills the size of your self esteem but vomit the appreciation people serve on your plate off handed. you write like chaos has possessed you and always spell your name along the syllables of mistakes and ruination.

you're a 10 but you always tend to count in negatives

—Saif Madre

I'm not an artist but

I'm not an artist but
my fingers are soaked red
of the corpse of my own imagination
a knife with sharp edges is my paintbrush
and my body a limitless canvas.
my mother braids grief in her hair
a hazy shade of muted blue
and my father tugs it hard
when she serves him disappointment for lunch
meanwhile i lay crouched, shivering in fear
a spectator of an early grave.
my best friend always taught me against
falling in love with a warning sign
but i am blind when it comes to green flags
and attached to those with rustel nails
stuck on their cold hearts.
shooting stars are perhaps a miracle
so is my forlorn gaze
when they fall on your amber eyes

amidst those fluttering eyelashes
but love lies on the tacky end
of a presumptuous fortune wheel
and I've never been one to be big on fates.
the sky is boundless they've said
and hope to be always counted on
but i breathe in shades of guilt
and lie hidden in drapes of grey
I'm not an artist but somehow
my apathy is rendered only perfectly
by the tip of my paintbrush.

—**Saif Madre**

i tell you i love you by

i. i am not a good conversationalist, but I'd tell you i love you by telling you how the world is cruel and the people flagstones of miseries, but despite it all, how we'd be synonyms for home to each other. that albeit the fact I'm clumsy around swords, i'd wield one if it's you that needs to be saved. i'd tell you if the world is a warzone, i'd always be your shelter, a safe space for you.

ii. i am not a good conversationalist, but I'd tell you I love you by leaving letters of reassurance next to your cup of tea with fortune cookies of our names combined. i'd lend a shoulder to your agony and intriguing squeals to even the trivial of your joys. i'd be companion to your silence, just somebody to lie in dark with, somebody's hand to touch.

iii. i am not a good conversationalist, but I'd tell you i love you by trying immensely to lessen the distance between our fond hearts, to hold tight the strings of fate conjuring us together. i'd listen to you pour your heart in cookie batters and squeeze a cup of vulnerability for a soup as warm as the love between us. i'd call you may it be payphones in desert or flip phones with crooked simcards. i'd whisper in your ears that our souls will be conjoined even if we are oceans apart.

iv. i am not a good conversationalist but i'd tell you how the only love language I'm fluent in is the truth. i'd destroy any evidence of forced promises lest it infest the edges of the raw love brewing among us. i'd build us a castle on bricks of honesty and cement our love in the colour of loyalty. i'd kiss you till the world around us melts and we are all that would matter.

v. i am not a good conversationalist but i'd make you origami of your favourite animals and make playlist with the titles of our favourite movies. i'd showcase my grand love by the monuments of little gestures and all of it to earn the redness of your cheeks and that star crossed look in your eyes. i'd do anything that would define our love into something finer than it has ever been.

I'm not a good conversationalist but of all the sentences I've managed to stutter, the one's with your names are as holy as i ever could be.

—Saif Madre

augusts bids a hard goodbye

time is still and the dewdrops on the mildew grass have forever been dissipated. there is a miserable illusion that comes along with the farewell of august, a lover's hug never embraced, a forbidden kiss stolen by the lips, a friend's betrayal and a stranger's recognition. august is slipping away and my hands are too heavy to hold it back.

there is a certain silence in the air and i can hear you breathing against my neck. you tell me the month is ending but it doesn't mean our love should and i cannot tell you how everything has a expiration date, love, most of all. august is the promise made at a funeral, ephemeral as the memories ever could be.

there is an unfinished poetry on your lips but I'm too shy to acknowledge them before you brush past me, our eyes an epithet of the religion we never believed in. i look at the metaphorical face of august and wonder of the time when we were here, entangled fingers and smiles with no efforts whatsoever. but time is irrelevant of teenage heartbreaks and the barks of trees don't bear carvings of our initials anymore.

august is the unreserved seats of half filled buses, the journey we were never meant to complete.

when i said i could be a romantic, you never told me cheesy poetries don't do the trick. for i have sonnets on your bedhead and odes to your bad breaths before breakfast but if you ask me to tell me of my love for you, i would stutter as if my tongue was as vestigial as my heart. august finds me reasons to stay with you but rationality was never one of your forte, was it?

my father told me always love was the devil's bait to the descending stairs of hell and i did not believe for my mother taught me always to live for the hope of it all. so when you knock on my door for the fourth time in a week, I'll let you in for second chances are a lover's compromise with the fates and august is slipping away but september makes promises august never meant to keep.

loving you was an apology i could never dare to make

we are sitting in the backseat of your car
your hand on my cheeks
and my eyes staring at yours
you tell me, with a snort of hesitation
"we cannot meet like this anymore."
and i want to cry and scream
and break the world apart
for all the misery it showered at us
with no mistake of our own.
if only forever was a book
i would've annotated it by your name
and preserve every page
where nobody could find us
you're the glimmering ray of hope
in my abode of darkness
and to be without you
is a staircase to hell
and i can't help but trip over.

now that we are going apart
should i tell you,
you're the only one
I'd fight these thunderstorms for
and you're the prayer
that ever made me believe in love
a love never to be exhausted.
so kiss me now like you could never again
and love me like you never stopped
for this is where the world would end
right here, with you and me.

—**Saif Madre**

you look like the one poets write about

my teacher asked me today
to find other words for home
but i doubt he would appreciate
if i wrote your arms over and over again
or would he watch with a disapproving glance
when i told him of your watercolour eyes
catching the attention of mine
with no efforts whatsoever.
i swear to the gods and demons
if i could describe love as a still image
it would be yours and yours alone
with your quirky smile spreading sunshine
and our hands held entwined
by the mere belief
even oceans couldn't drown us
for we have already sunk rock bottom
in a love so priceless.
when you look at me with all the love

the universe could keep at your feet
i can't help but feel grateful
to be able to look in your eyes
and call you mine
for in no world i believed i could find someone so beautiful
someone who looks like the one poets write about.

—Saif Madre

if i could tell you the long version of the story

if i could tell you the long version of the story
our story, i wouldn't
for i am not so unkind
to have you wallow in shame and guilt
and stutter apologies like chants
of a god you never cared for enough.
i could not have you cry and scream
for all the misery you caused
with every kiss you took from me
perhaps my agony was too transparent
for your drunk bloody eyes
or maybe you could never look beyond
the quicksand of pity you were drowning in
to realize you were sabotaging
the only life jacket holding you up.
everytime you told me it was love
when you left bruises between my eyes
i believed you nonchalantly

for that was what love looked like
that was how my parents loved
but sometimes turning a blind eye
would hurt a little more than before
and wrapping myself in the blanket of death
seemed easier than to be "loved" by you.
a priest once told me
to know my demons by name
so i cut my wrists by satan's blade
and drowned in my own blood
chanting your name as if
you were the god i cared for
more than enough to kill me.

—**Saif Madre**

the things I keep to remember you on purpose

i. the bracelet i promised I'd never wear

love is shaky, nothing like the movies show with a bundle of love sewn by the strings of unbreakable oaths. it ages with time and only those who do not oppose growth survive it, unlike us. our love was a calamity and us the unnecessary collateral damage, but among all the ruins I've kept a reminder of you among the beads I've wrapped around my wrist.

ii. your broken round glasses

the world is a terrible place but even storms looked a little like rainbows when i looked at them through your eyes. a quick visit through the memory lane along the dusty closets got me familiar to your glasses which you found too nerdy for your good. but i always liked them, more on you but to find them collecting dust in the big box of bursting nostalgia granted me a closure i once reckoned impossible.

iii. the plastic orchids that would never wilt

i still remember the day to my core when you came rushing to me with those plastic flowers to my great dismay. obvious of my disappointment, you explained how real flowers may wilt but these will live everyday, a constant reminder of our eternal love. a disbelieving look from me made you tell me how you were too broke to buy the real ones, but still i think everyday, was that why we broke apart? was our love too real to survive?

iv. the jumper that smells like us

it is no surprise that i'd give anything to hold you, have our fingers intertwined under a sky full of stars, find the abode for an outcast like me in those brown eyes, to keep a forever apart where we would choose each other every time with no second thoughts. but desires are often left incomplete, and all that I've closest to you is the yellow sweater you'd wear and lie in my arms, the sweater that defined love for us.

v. broken clocks that didn't survive the wounds of time

everyone has different interests, so did you. yours was antiques, aside from me obviously. you'd always take me to museums and buy clocks that you'd adorn the walls of your room with. sometimes i too would save money to get you one but the last one i bought for you didn't reach you before we fell apart. you returned it to me with a note that maybe i should return it and get the moneh back, but i didn't have the courage to do so. so it sits on the countertop, broken but still ticking the time we both lost.

vi. love letters sans any love

did i ever let you know how your handwriting always made my heart jump a little. there were a stack of love notes you always left for me but all they are now is a cue of how i wouldn't find any more hidden in my locker or tucked in the pockets of my oversized jackets you always liked to steal. but perhaps the universe is too witty to let me indulge in my misery alone, for i get a text from you. you remembered the date, i notice and i cry into a heap of nostalgia unlooked for. unwilling to hold back, i respond to you.
"saif, do you still love me?"
"i wish, i didn't."

—Saif Madre

and i beg you

and i beg you
please, do not take me home
if it's not in your arms
please, forget my name
if you wouldn't call it gently
like you always did
slowly, like cherries on your lips
a syllable at time, in sync with
rhythms of our unsteady love.
it might be considered foolish
that i do not remember what
my life was ever if not you
what did my fingers do
if not caress the locks of your hair
what names did my lips remember
if not the sweet melody of yours.
the universe has given signs time and again
that we aren't meant to be alone
and our constellations are aligned

fated to be together
and i wish i could tell you
in so many words
everything i know about love
starts and ends by you
but i am helpless
so helpless in love.
there are raw etchings on my ribcage
your initials with pink hearts
blind to the naked eye
scribbled poetries and intimate conversations
you're moonlight personified
with star studded eyes
our love is a religion even atheists worship
for i might be an apologist
but loving you was never one of my regrets.

—Saif Madre

are you here?

"are you here? did you leave yet?" i called your name out in small whispers reeking of helplessness. a sudden rumble from across the room calmed my nerves. you were there, i realised. peace washed over me when you called out my name in weak syllables, your voice the only melody holy to my ears. you were the peace the world needed but only i had.

fates are questionable when you believe in them too much. i prayed to god so much but it was perhaps satan who cared to answer. i told them everything of you, your eyes bright like sunshine and the comfort embedded in your every touch, the citrus smiles and the tangerine like sarcasm, bittersweet and delicate. i told satan that i loved you so much, that if the bridges break apart, your face was the last one I'd want to remember.

but was it my bad luck that a new volume of archie's comics did not reach the pits of hell every week that satan took my wishes too literal for it to be adorned in my plateau of metaphors. that one fine day, we were travelling by a bus you weren't very keen on boarding but anyway did for me. destiny, if you may call it, toppled over the bus over the bridge and so many travellers trekked a journey to the skies above. us? we weren't mortally injured but the beautiful metaphor cost me my two eyes and you, a early ticket to orphanage.

we were heart broken but the absence of my vision did not ignite my grief as much as the guilt did. it was no surprise you loved your parents so much that the grief was now running in your veins, too tangible to be ever forgotten. i wanted to tell you the truth, but i didn't know if you'd understand that underneath the sin, lied a heart unretriveably in love with you.

but i knew you deserved to know the truth. i could not take away the choice from you, to hate me or not. i told you, in small whispers, your hand was in mine, nervous from the words you were hearing. you were a rational person but i didn't know how much the tragedy broke you apart. i saw you hesitate, loosen your hand from mine and slivers of my heart dipped in the agony of what i did. there were a lot of tears i didn't see, but felt when they fell on my arms but as soon i was getting ready to let you go, you took me in your embrace and broke apart. i liked that you needed me, that your head needed my shoulder to rest on.

"you were always a good story teller." you said. and i didn't know if to convince you it's the truth or be selfish and bask in your love. i didn't want you to love me with a delusion but as i started to say, you put a finger on my lips and told me you understand and forgive me if that's what i need. i nod my head in a moment of joy and you interrupt it by kissing me. your lips taste like the saudade i never imagined i would've. i could not see you but as the devil promised it was only your face i remembered, only yours for a borrowed eternity.

"saif, will you stay the night?"
"you're the only home I'm left with."

—Saif Madre

love is not a feeling but a metaphor

//for longing hearts and unsaid confessions// for promises on sand, ephemeral as ever// for the hundred glimpses we shared in a lingering eye contact// for shaky hands picking up shards of our heart// for a crimson dream where you lay beside me// a metaphor for days when you're all mine.

//for torn pages of romantic novellas// for the taylor swift songs strumming through the earphones// for the love letters we never wrote with our blood// for the disguise of sarcasm when honesty is too heavy to bear// for lopsided grins and starry eyes// a metaphor for a home in your arms.

//for tangerine dreams and ardent desires// for delicate embraces and soft kisses// for reading under the sunset and dancing in the rain// for paper rings and plucked flowers// for whispering disclosures of love on an unmade bed// for your face cupped between my hands// for tucking your hair behind your ears// a metaphor for little gestures and grand love.

//for different love languages entwined together// for defining our love on our own// for reading poetry and reciting lines// for watching shows together till we yawn// for the semblance of pride in their eyes// for awaited 11:11 and whispering sweet nothings// a metaphor for being together even when miles apart.

—**Saif Madre**

it's 3:03 am on a school night

it's 3:03 am on a school night
and you're in your father's car
knowing he'd be angry when he knows
but the world is so much bigger
than your father's spilling rage
and your teenage escapades.
it's 3:08 am on a school night
and you're in your father's car
holding hands with a boy
with blue, blue eyes
and freckles straight out of a rom-com
he promises you always and forever
and you believe him because love never lies.
it's 3:15 am on a school night
and you're in your father's car
you're kissing him in the backseat
and you wonder why you didn't yet
his lips are bittersweet and delicate
almost the taste of love.

it's 3:30 am on a school night
and you're in your father's car
your lips are sore from all the kissing
and you realise he is reaching for your clothes
maybe he doesn't see the way you hesitate
maybe he does and ignores it
you resist and firmly say no
he looks at you with disappointment
and murmurs something that rhymes to your no.
it's 9:18 am on a school day
and you just got out of your dad's car
but something is strange
in the way everyone looks at you
it doesn't take long for you to register
when you find your locker spray painted slut
and a reputation ruined because someone's ego was too big.
it's 2:12 pm on a school day
and your dad's car is parked behind your school
waiting to pick you up
because you punched the guy
with blue blue eyes and romantic freckles
before screaming you weren't some princess turned slut he can rule over
but a dame with a sword longer than his....

except you cannot complete the sentence
before being pulled over.
it's 3:03 pm
and you're in your father's car
an ice cream treat before reaching home
his way of saying he is proud of you.

hey, the city is crying and i miss you

hey, the city is crying and i miss you
more than i can bear
except we are strangers now
the broken remains of our illicit affair
summer died in your arms
but your freckles still shine bright
my jumper still smells of your cologne
scattered memories of our last night
i am mourning for my younger self
so hopelessly in love with you
but pity has never been my love language
rebellion was all i ever knew.
i liked the way you say things
whispering sweet nothings in my ears
never knew when you became a habit
that would soon leave me in tears
you showed me the difference between grasping and holding

but all i knew was to cling to your life
my chest feels empty now sans your embrace
so i fulfill your absence with blunt knives
acceptance looks different on everybody
a pathetic bonnet on my tainted shirt
pretenses are my only best friends
a heavenly mirage in my endless desert.
someday perhaps we'd meet again
and love wouldn't feel so tough
an impromptu clash in grocery aisles
our lingering glances to be enough.

—Saif Madre

the world is a canvas and god is a shoddy artist

silence churns in the dimlit room of an apartment close to demolishing. an old mother cooks for her son who is asleep on the cold floor, a rag for a metaphor of warmth. the mother is dying but believes her sinking life line is not worth the suffocating hospital bills. the son is oblivious and hardworking but fates plays tricks he never asked for. but every evening when the son returns, the mother lays out the dinner and share a laugh or two and everything feels as bright as it ever could be.

across them, in a tower with glass windows live a family of four. blessed with every materialistic joy, they wake up at 12 at noon to the sound of housemaid ringing the bell and breakfast in beds. but what lies in the web of perfection are leeches of bitter truth. the father lives more on business trips than their home and the mother loves to hold a cigar more than she ever did her child's hands.

the twins feed on disappointment for lunch and only thing they know for a family is a stray dog too much of a hazard to bring to their perfect house.

if love had claws sharper than a shrapnel's edge, we'd be living in a never ending warzone and counting massacres if not years. so believes the brown eyed boy living in the guest room of his best friend's house because his parents were too proud to accept his painted nails and love for another guy. "god would send you to hell." they said, but he knows in the deepest corners of his heart that the burning daggers could never inflict so much pain as the one stabbed by those he believed loved him.

there is a strange odour that encapsulates the air and people may say it's the hospital environment but he knows it's his sweater that's reeking of spilled soup and striped pyjamas he forgot to change on his way to the hospital. it's the third day of his wedding and while they were supposed to be on a cruise, but only if he woke up at time and went to the grocery store to get milk so she wouldn't have to, she may not have slipped from the stairs and be hanging from the thread of life, mere steps away from the doors of death.

prayers echo in the halls of the god but the only poetry dearest to him is of grief and tragedy.

loving you could never be a mistake

and perhaps when everything goes to hell
when the earth bursts open
and the once colourful trees
are now a heap of ash on the ground
when the rage of God destroys
all in their mere sight
i am inclined to believe that
my love for you would survive
for its 49 months since we talked
but your name still stirs
the dead butterflies in my stomach
and my lips could never forget
the taste of yours.
i still remember when we were walking
on that yellow brick road
and i pulled you towards me
our eyes held in a glance
i could never tell you

how much i loved you then
the flutter of your eyelashes
the crease of your lopsided smile
i would kiss you if i could
for a little hope never hurt
when it's about you, only you.
i always wanted to ask the mercy of God
why do you love him? and not me?
why does our story have to end terribly
locked lips for a unsteady closure
time, the uncertain antagonist
but if everything falls into place someday
and love is still our undying catalyst
knock my door thrice and I would know
for loving you could never be a mistake
for loving you is all i know.

—**Saif Madre**

sometimes i say everything's okay but

sometimes i say everything's okay but i have been choking on my dried tears for month's and yet i cannot help but smile when someone greets me. i am aware things will be okay alright and there's a rainbow at the end of the tunnel but the metaphorical dagger stuck in me is yet too painful to be forgotten by the salvation of hope. sometimes i say everything's okay but the pretentiousness is the only truth i now believe in.

sometimes i say everything's okay but i write letters to my dead mother and cry over graves devoid any flowers. i wonder, when i die, will people care of my absence? did i make a difference in the world or was i a stepping stone to be thrown into dirty ponds.

sometimes i say everything's okay but i am starting to believe death is as questionable as my existence.

sometimes i say everything's okay but there is a forbidden kiss on my lips i could never manage to erase even if i wanted to. a memory too pure to ever be tainted, a guilt beautiful enough to never regret. love may be a fool's errand but what is humanity if not dumb mistakes and decisions of heart. sometimes i say everything's okay but love always will taste like her lips.

sometimes i say everything's okay but there is a hollow feeling in my chest from all the love that's lacking from my heart. i look at people with a steady sense of belonging and wish it were me too. words are futile devices, incapable to express my ardent desire to be held and never let go. sometimes i say everything's okay but i want to have someone to stay with me for once.

sometimes i say everything's okay but suffering now seems like a language in itself and i envy those illiterate of it. misery is tangled in my fingers and there is melancholy tucked between my eyelids. sometimes i am scared that i may not survive the high tide of pain, drowning helplessly with no hand to pull me up again. *sometimes i say everything's okay but nothing is.*

—Saif Madre

hey with the intention of

hey(with the intention of talking to you everyday so you fall for me too. whispering sudden i love you's on call so your cheeks fluster red as you sleep. making impromptu appearances in your dreams and daydreams alike. looking deep in your eyes till our souls brush against each other and your hands are familiar to the slight brush of mine).

hey(with the intention of taking you on a date along the railway platform running behind trains. gifting you a crayon box hoping you'd colour our love someday. writing a poem for the god that starts by the syllables of your name. wasting so many days in the impossible pursuit of your forbidden love).

hey(with the intention of taking care of you like no one ever did before. gatekeeping the sound of your laugh covered in sunshine. whispering sweet nothings in your ears for the days you can't pull yourself together. being the reason your face is always curled up in a smile).

hey(with the intention of bullying and teasing you till you get angry. bringing you your favourite chocolate just to look at you jump in joy. accompanying you to our quick escapades at an attempt to window shopping. maintaining the eye contact till both of us blush. looking at you and knowing what love looks like).

—Saif Madre

our love has become a memory too bitter to reminiscence

on my fourteenth day of therapy, my therapist asked me what words do i associate with the emotion love and all i can think of is hate and neglect. i try to be optimistic but it's love that has drawn curtains over all the brightness of my life. i want to tell her how loving is a curse dipped in honeycombs and all of us have a sweet tooth bigger than the sizes of our brain but all i tell her is love makes me think of you.

everyday you come back home tired and our eyes catch a glance, the reeking odour of our dead love is strong enough to suffocate me. everytime our lips touch, all i can hear is the humming of our romantic obligations. there is a sweet toothed lie we have lived everyday but never speak of,

for we are next to each other yet worlds apart;

promising a forever of estranged hearts

one of these days we will part ways, a flagstone of a fullstop in a ravine of commas but i look at you and wish that perhaps god would let us be together one more day, give a chance to ignite the fire wood of the love we once burned together with marshmallows to roast. we may be known strangers now but there is a string of affinity that the devil vowed never to snip. do i like you? not anymore. but i worship you for you were the only god who ever held my shaking hands.

if this was a love poem

if this was a love poem
I would be writing about you and me
that one epic love in nine lives
perfect as it ever may be.
words, an imperfect medium
lasting glances of our longing eyes
I would speak of my open heart
the smile you gave, my precious prize.
if holiness was an image
it would be the portait of you
entangled fingers and lips locked
under a sky, cloudy and blue.
a quick walk under the bridge
adorned by hanging misletoe
kissing in the name of love
wishing we'd never let go.
if this was a love poem
i would be writing about you and me
i don't know much about forever
but i think it is what are we.

glimpses of us (saif's version)

i met a girl, despite myself. in the dusty aisles of the oldest library, our hands touched the same pages of torn literature, a weak smile and awkward conversation. she was the poet's religion and a misogynist's worst nightmare, a landmark on the map of perfect little things. i met a girl who i could take out but she wasn't you.

i met a girl with frizzy blond hair and round rimmed glasses she never took off. her fingers felt like cotton candy and her eyes the keyhole to the third floor of paradise. we talked on calls in the evenings and met before sun touched the horizon again. we shared bubblegum ice-cream and held hands on walks and called when midnight was too lonely to be awake at. i met a girl i could love but she wasn't you.

it is a shame how we are miles apart but everytime i kiss her, it's your lips that kiss me back. our held hands speaks too much poetry that holding hers seems no much than a whisper. she hugs me when she is scared by horror movies and complains when i forget to call back but everytime she says i love you, it's your voice i hear.

love is a fool's errand so everytime she calls me to come over i burn the letters you never wrote me and burn our photos that i stashed hoping you'd come back. i accept forgetting you will never be an option so i let you go. i take her on dates where we kissed and paint new initials on the walls where we painted ours. i tell her about you but don't leave out the fact that it's her I'll choose now.

i met a girl who's not you but that's what i love about her.

—Saif Madre

love looks a lot like

i. spending time together

before i met you, my life was a haze of moments running away from each other, a survival i was not so fond of. until we crossed paths in that empty train, two stations away from my destination. out of habit, i took a book out that i have already read, and you quoted my favourite lines, as i looked at your freckled face with an arc of the heaven for a smile. words exchanged, so did numbers and making excuses i skipped my station only to spend a little more time with you. then, love looked a lot like stupid sacrifices for the sake of you.

ii. holding hands and stolen gazes.

some would say we were going fast when you didn't hesitate in holding my hands when i introduced you to my friends, but you always knew what was the right thing to do at the right time. you were a surprising visitor at my self arranged exile and it was by you i knew how living was better than surviving the day. before i knew, we were stealing glances across the room and love absolutely looked like sheepish grins when our eyes met.

iii. unsteady confessions under the stars

while i am very well known for my stammering words and breaking confidence, when you didn't mind sitting with me at the doctor's for a delayed appointment, i somehow knew it would be foolish to ever let you go. so under a not so well constructed excuse of star gazing, i took you on a (maybe?) date where the universe would be witness to my bewitching love for you. but being me, i could not utter the words till you asked, "do you want to go out with me, on a date?" and i couldn't help but nod repeatedly as you chuckled. love, at that moment, looked a lot like wishes on shooting stars and possible first dates.

iv. knowing each other better.

our long walks from home to the bus station were sometimes silent and often crazy with words where you told me all about you and i listened because you were the book i wanted to read a thousand times over, the song on loop, the movie that never gets boring. when i told you i like flowers, you brought a bouquet of the prettiest one's and told me they reminded you of me. being with you, love looked like my flustered cheeks, for which you were to be blamed.

v. concluding arguements with "i love you's"

as human we were, we were bound to disagree sometime. so when you skipped our dates a few times, it upset me to a certain degree. but afraid I'd seem annoying, i never complained anything to you, sealing my silences with an expression of annoyance. you noticed and asked if anything was wrong and after i told you after a long time of convincing and fighting, you apologised but asked me to tell you if anything happens rather than keeping it burdened. after an icecream date, love looked a lot like apologetic smiles and brushing icecream off your chin.

vi. making you my home

this weekend, while cleaning my mother found the love letters you wrote me stashed carefully in the closet. showing them to me, she asked me about you and while i couldn't be more scared, i knew the only way out of this was honesty. i told her all about you and she asked me if you make me happy and i told her, "more than i could ever imagine." she smiled with her all knowing eyes and hugged me, whispering in my ears, "don't let her go, she seems a keeper." and i since then, love never stopped looking like you.

—**Saif Madre**

i wish i could love you, i really do

of all the days
you look deep in my eyes
searching for a glimpse of love,
i wish i could tell you
there is something to look for
there is something to yearn
from this bandaged heart of mine
surviving on rusted nails of hope,
for if murder is cathartic
loving me is an empty space with eerie silences.
you do not understand
that it isn't just your heart
that burns with every confession
but so does mine
when i put away my only chance
to ever sincerely be loved
for all the polaroids i burned of you
the memories never fails to remind

and every good in goodbyes i said
was a apology i was too scared to offer.
i wish i could love you, i really do
for we were given the stars, you and i,
but the apocalypse struck
before our lips could ever touch.

—**Saif Madre**

what's love?

//love is teenage dreams and big mistakes// love is God's favourite knife stabbed in your Achilles heel// love is looking them in the eyes and not blinking// love is closed eyes and minute long hugs// love is wishing on dandelions and crying when they don't come true// love is knowing it's miserable but still pining for it//

//love is paper hearts and rings made of rose stems// love is being an atheist and yet calling them your religion// love is annotated books and whispered i love you's in their backyard// love is the confession you never needed to make//

love is counting lifetimes you would be with them// love is not wanting those where you don't get them embraced in your arms// love is looking for someone to fall for your whole life and yet falling at the most unexpected times// love is holding on when the life is falling apart// love is staying even when the house is on fire//

//love is bringing them wildflowers because you were too broke to buy a bouquet//love is them saying, they like this better anyways//

love is clementine cheeks and stolen glances followed by giggles// love is kisses on the forehead and hands held for an impending eternity//

—**Saif Madre**

do you miss me too?

i used to think of all the things we could be but strangers wasn't what i expected. of all the times i thought love was a faraway dream never written for me, you did things and said words that told me otherwise. im sitting on my kitchen floor with a broken bottle of hot sauce by the floor because spotify played your favourite song and all i can think about is how you wanted us to dance together on it until you didn't. i have a hundred things to tell you but all i hear from your end is utter silence, as if all you ever said with my name in the end, was a cry to get away, to leave and never look back. never ever.

you always said love was a tricky business and if I'd listened to you, I'd not be drowning in the debts of all the love you never cared to reciprocate. for every time you called me your sun, i was too distracted by your star studded eyes to ever hear you say it's the darkness that allures you. we would sleep on calls every night and i don't think i have smiled as much as i did since then. i think every time I'd never talk to you again if you reached out but even in dreams, i'd melt to hear you call my name, a whisper even.

do you miss me too?

do you miss me like i miss you?

—**Saif Madre**

pretty pretty boys

pretty pretty boys have apologies stuck in their gums for sins they never committed// pretty pretty boys are a gasping mess and nickname themselves a burden// pretty pretty boys tuck flowers behind their ears and paint their nails the colour of sky// pretty pretty boys look like they could devour themselves whole//

pretty pretty boys has scars on their knuckles by punching walls// pretty pretty boys stay up at till 3 am to write poetry about a girl they never met// pretty pretty boys eat scrambled eggs for breakfast but are still hungry for the look of pride in their father's eyes// pretty pretty boys scribble on the last page of their notebook but tear it lest anyone would read//

pretty pretty boys have a smile brighter than the sun and a frown deep enough to drown a kraken// pretty pretty boys worship silence as if it were a god and lay wilted roses on the grave of their tenderness// pretty pretty boys hide behind curtains and dug their face in the crevices of the ribs of a best friend with a heart warm enough// pretty pretty boys believes everyone would be better off without them//

pretty pretty boys never smoke but their lips taste like ash and there is an emptiness in their eyes// pretty pretty boys find their abode in the aisle of a bookstore, sipping coffee and reading away// pretty pretty boys water dead plants and chants their grief hoping it would go away// pretty pretty boys have a leg hanging in the past to ever embrace the present// pretty pretty boys live memories more than scenarios//

pretty boys never really believe they're pretty

—Saif Madre

you are more divine than the stars ever could be.

the clock is ticking and the world is somehow slower than i have ever seen it be. all is well until my eyes find a glimpse of the constellations secured beneath your wary eyelashes. i cannot help but stare as you take steps towards me and i would be lying if i said i didn't have the urge to hold your hand and dance at the middle of the airport, except i had wobbly feet and you'd be snoring the very few seconds your head rest on my shoulders.

you wake up to a breakfast in bed prepared by yours truly with a note to be prepared for all the adventures the day could bring for you, while I'm standing right there looking at your cheeks turn pink. with an hour or two to spare, you get ready and despite my reluctance, i blabber,

"you look so beautiful....darling."

"don't call me that."

"okay......"

"No."

"....sweetheart."

and people still ask me how I ended up with a bruised arm yet a enlightened and apparently pink face from all that smiling.

on the trip to the bookstore, i click random photos of you reading books that you already have at your kingdom of a bookshelf while you look at me now and then with a hint of modest eyes yet the narcissism glinting bright as the glory of sun from your big brown eyes. you tell me i cannot buy you anything you haven't read before and i ask you if you're sure as i pull a notebook out with your name written all over it and poetries scribbled of you as their muse.
"still, you didn't buy it." you say
and i stand there, rolling my eyes as you chuckle and hug the notebook, as if you'd never let it go.

what better could be the end to a day than to lie under the stars and look at them as we talk of things as mundane as the colour of my curtain and your makeup hacks which i swore i wouldn't tell anyone.
"what if we were made of stardust?" you asked.
"i think we are. maybe it's what makes every person so beautiful."
"so, if I'm made of stardust, does that make me a star?" you ask grinning when i stare in your eyes for a short second before leaning in and whispering in your ears,
"you are more divine than the stars ever could be."

—Saif Madre

darling, i'd give you the sun.

hold my hand and
let's walk to the stars
I'd sing you my favourite song
and let you play the guitar.
tell me you love me
and i'd always prove you right
in a world drowning in darkness
I'd be your ever glowing light.
we are starbucks lovers
but as broke one could be
you have the flecks in your eyes
a glimpse of home, when you look at me.
draw me in red crayon
splotches of unused paint
forget being an ugly muse
if you're the god, i'd be your saint.
we are dancing at midnight
amid the paris of nowhere
you kiss me on my lips

red cheeks, an everlasting stare.
and when we dance, hands in hand
you look like god's favourite religion
so give me the stars you've been holding on
and darling, i'd give you the sun.

—**Saif Madre**

grief is your mother tongue, still you bite your tongue talking of it

you're sitting alone on the cold floor, knocking your knuckles against the kitchen cabinets. you hope to hear a voice, a cry for help so you can hold a hand and pull it to the surface, while your feet are almost drowning. you have caution burned in your skin but you're too reckless to ever think about yourself. you want to call it saviour complex but all you ever do is self sabotage. you want to save the world and lit a match on your kerosene poured body at the same time.

you never believe the world exists also for you. you tell everyone you want to be the background character in a movie, and a name lost between a hundred pages but the truth is, you believe that's what you'll ever be. you feel its ridiculous that someone would look in your eyes and never look away, that someone would kiss your lips not for pity but because they want to. it's been a long time you're feeling alone, but you'd rather die then hold someone's hand long enough, scared they'll let go the moment you tighten the fingers. you're feeling helpless but never call for it, you're desperate but your casual smile never gives the secret away.

of all the day you burn the last pages of your diary, you write your name on the first one. your friends want you to go out with them, but the world changes across the street, it's more cruel, it stares and pricks on the pretentious confidence you've moulded, a consolation prize in a pottery contest. you cry your dead mother's tears which you never got to wipe, and your hearts slipping off the greasy sleeves with so many heads leaning. your therapist asks you of the pain loss makes you feel, and you tell her even your screams are void of any voice. you tell her how grief is your mother tongue but you still bite your tongue talking of it.

—Saif Madre

the world is collapsing and we have the front row tickets

we are in the middle of an apocalypse
trees strewn around
a hurricane in my throat
you are clenching my hands
and I'm looking into your eyes
as if we are in a manic pixie dream
the only survivors in a heap of destruction
the only lovers in a crowd of corpses.
if i could, I'd make you the eye of the storm
where god's rage is a hint of thunder
and his mercy floods civilizations
i bandage your scraped knees
and you kiss me on my cheeks
eyes closed, horrors forgotten
we are in a new world now
made from stardust in a pickle jar
and leftover poetry with unsteady rhymes

you tell me you want us to start over
but the world is collapsing
and we have the front row tickets.

—**Saif Madre**

we are the amalgamations of our worst mistakes and bittersweet memories

look me in the eyes and tell me we have lost the war of love, that the corpses of our past selves sliced a knife through their ways for nothing, that a promise is a sin in delay and that god would take offense that we paid a visit to the altar of satan and called it our petty mistakes. I still have the half burnt polaroids we clicked drunk and miserable, when you told me if love was forbidden, *you'd shamelessly be a rebel for me* and I chuckled looking at the moon shining from your eyes. your blue plaid shirt still smells like the black coffee I spilled on you and I am yet reeking of the apologies I was too scared to make.

if time was holy, god turned his back on us when we needed him the most

no but, your name is an undying reminder of the purple magnolia flowers in my garden and spotify has claws lunged in my ribcages for every playlist you ever made for me. I swear the world stops spinning when I hear someone call your name and I peel angst off my chest and stuff it in places no one would ever look. my collar bones are nostalgic of the time you spilled some love over them and I want to ask you when could I return the favour except we changed our paths at a crossroad and the universe knows better than to intercept our paths again.

love will always be my miserable excuse to hold your hand again.

—Saif Madre

love was a sin forgotten over burnt breakfast

oh to be somebody's muse, a wonder carved on raw papyrus, blood scrawled across the canvas, a lover's myth, a prejudice too holy. you call me at 3 am on a stormy night and say that the hurricane is going to devour the world alone, and while I should hang up on you like you always did, my fingers are trembling and my mouth is dry for I haven't heard of you since we fell apart one sunny morning, when love was a sin forgotten over burnt breakfast. i have wilted flowers left at my doorstep, a letter reeking of unmade apologies for words could never encompass all the grief you made me feel when you left. you ask me if I would let you back in my life, and I really want to say yes except I am used to the emptiness that comes with sitting penniless in a phone booth. you tell me I have changed and I tell you it was the act of unloving you that made me. you ask me to give you another chance but I chuckle for I have run out of chances and a heart to love again. perhaps we were once meant to be, but there a lot of forevers and this one isn't for us.

a heavy consequence of god's worst mistakes

you are running barefoot in a city made of broken glass and spattered with blood and sweat, for in this moment, fearless as to all your stupid ventures are wars you never lost and your rebellion is a sweet sorrow you have grown a taste for. you want to take the world by it's collar, drag it's sludgy feet across the mud, a metaphor for your dirty vengeance. you're angry at the world for your mother's early death and a crippling anxiety forming in your jaw everytime you look at someone familiar. your vulnerability is a noose to your falling apart sanity but a few tears are the price of a thousand nails pushed into the body of a forgotten god. when you stare hard at the mirror, you can see your chipped naivety around your nails and a innocence forged in a soul lost and forgotten. you tell yourself that you're fighting but all you find yourself to be is a heavy consequence of god's worst mistakes.

you call me your muse but I'm just a disaster

we are in the empty halls, chasing time as it runs away, slips from our palms as if we never held it. we can feel the walls closing in on us, the floor is shaking and the ceiling has cracks on it, threatening to fall apart. i look at you, a final look of yearning, a glance into your brown eyes and it shimmers like a star long forgotten. your lips hold a reckoning and i am too oblivious of judgements to not kiss them.

we are standing in the court, marrying off our best friends, a witness of their undying love but blind to our own struggles. we are staying the night in an old hotel room and of all the romcoms we once watched together, fate plays the one bed trope card on us with a hint of maniacal laugh. silence devours our space alone and the thought cuts me into pieces, that how things will always be like this.

it's midnight when i wake up to the sound of your sobs. perhaps you were reading urdu poetry about heartbroken lovers like us, or a craving for bagels hit you right in the gut like always. i want to ask you but to take your name would be like awakening a false god i never stopped worshipping. i know you better than i do myself, so much that i could translate your soul in languages i have never learnt and write you an ode to the crease on your nose when you laugh like there is no tomorrow. love is a bitter remembrance of memories tainted by petty heartbreaks.

but when we leave the next day, perhaps we would never see each other again. we would go paths in different ways, never to intertwine in a hundred centuries. so i don't mind, when you pull me aside in an empty room of eerie silences but beating hearts. you smell of stale liquor and cheap candies bought at confectionery stalls. hours later, we are apart but your touch lingers on me so much that it's tangible. you told me you're a poet now, writing of tragedies and love as a detonation and someday I'd be a subject of all the love you had left on you. you tell me of everything you love about me and all i hear is a voice i can't believe.

you call me your muse, but i tell you I'm just a disaster

—Saif Madre

---

they say its a sin to love,
to look deep into someone's eyes
and call them your god.
to blush a carnal red when they smile at you. to have your heart in a platter
and serve them with a sip of your blood.
to romanticise the tension in the room
when you are both alone together
to kiss in those empty silences,
fingers intertwined, a holy embrace.
they say its a sin to love
but you wouldn't mind hell if they're next to you.

—Saif Madre

a poet's worst muse is themselves

did you know? that when a poet writes of tragedy, their most humane urge is to forget it. to let the words burn on the paper and not their fractured hearts. to have a break from the excruciating pain of being, to waver off the sorrow hidden beneath bitten fingernails. of all the nights i get dreams of my dead mother, she is very much alive. she knows my name, speaks it like a lullaby. i want to hold her voice and clench my fingers on her embrace, knowing there would be darkness when i open my eyes. the world is a sinning ground but here we are the saints with broken hearts. you still think of your estranged lover as if they never left. you worship apologies on the shrine of indifference but gods don't believe in last chances. you write poetries of love and say they're fictional, but the scars on your palms still grieve the hands they once held.

—Saif Madre

www.ingramcontent.com/pod-product-compliance
Lightning Source LLC
LaVergne TN
LVHW091259150826
845673LV00006B/1469

* 9 7 9 8 8 8 8 8 3 9 1 2 6 *